NEW COLLECTED POEMS

Tomas Tranströmer
NEW COLLECTED POEMS

translated by Robin Fulton

BLOODAXE BOOKS

ISBN: 1 85224 413 5

First published 1997 by
Bloodaxe Books Ltd,
P.O. Box 1SN,
Newcastle upon Tyne NE99 1SN.

Bloodaxe Books Ltd acknowledges
the financial assistance of Northern Arts.

Cover printing by J. Thomson Colour Printers Ltd, Glasgow.

Printed in Great Britain by
Cromwell Press Ltd, Broughton Gifford, Melksham, Wiltshire.

Contents

BELLS AND TRACKS (1966)

SEEING IN THE DARK (1970)

FOR LIVING AND DEAD (1989)

THE SAD GONDOLA (1996)

MEMORIES LOOK AT ME (1993)

Acknowledgements

This collection contains all the poems which Tomas Tranströmer has published in book form, plus a few more recent pieces.

It is an expanded version of his *Collected Poems*, published by Bloodaxe Books in 1987, to which I have added translations of Tomas Tranströmer's later collections *For Living and Dead* (1989) and *The Sad Gondola* (1996), as well as his prose memoir, *Memories Look at Me*, first published in *Contemporary Authors: Autobiography Series*, edited by Joyce Nakamura (Gale Research, Inc., Detroit: vol.17, 1993). An earlier selection of thirty-six poems was published by Penguin Books in 1974. Then in 1981 Ardis Books (Ann Arbor) brought out a bigger selection, this time containing ninety poems, plus the complete *Baltics*, and with the addition of an interview originally recorded with Gunnar Harding in 1973.

Most of the translations published here have already appeared, either in magazines or in booklets, and acknowledgements are due to: *The American-Scandinavian Review* (USA), *Antaeus* (USA), *Cave* (New Zealand), *Contemporary Literature in Translation* (Canada), *The Fiction Magazine, Field* (USA), *Frank* (France), *Genre* (USA), *Inside Sweden* (Sweden), *The Irish Times, Ironwood* (USA), *The Journal of Contemporary Scandinavian Poetry, Kenyon Review* (USA), *Lines Review, London Magazine, Manhattan Review* (USA), *Modern Poetry in Translation, Ninth Decade, Oasis, Planet, Poesie Europe* (Germany), *Poetry Review, Poetry Wales, Scandinavian Review* (USA), Sceptre Press, *Second Aeon, Spirit* (USA), *Stand, Swedish Book Review, Telegram, The Times Literary Supplement, Toronto Life, 2PLUS2* (Switzerland), *World Literature Today* (USA) and *Verse*. Poems, singly or in groups, have also been in books published by: Dedalus Press (Dublin), Ecco Press (NY), Edinburgh University Press, Faber & Faber, St Martin's Press (Boston, Mass), The Swedish Institute (Stockholm) and White Pine Press (Fredonia, NY).

Many of the translations in this collection have been revised since their previous appearance, and I would particularly like to record my thanks to Tomas Tranströmer himself for his unfailing help over the years.

The cover picture by Sirkka-Liisa Konttinen, *Snow Angel*, is from the photographic project *My Finnish Roots* and the documentary film *Letters to Katja*.

Introduction

Tomas Tranströmer was born in Stockholm in 1931. Since 1954 he has published eleven collections of poems whose qualities are such that for the past forty years he has been one of the most highly regarded figures in contemporary Swedish poetry. He is also one of the most-translated of living Swedish poets. As well as shorter selections published in over forty languages, larger selections have appeared in Spanish, Dutch, Hungarian, German, French, and of course English. American poets who have translated his work include Robert Bly, Samuel Charters and May Swenson. There is a large and growing body of critical articles and interviews scattered in many periodicals and newspapers, and among books on Tranströmer we should mention Kjell Espmark's substantial study of 1983 (*Resans formler / The Journey's Formulae*) and Lennart Karlström's very detailed bibliography of 1990 (soon to be updated).

Up to 1990 Tranströmer worked as a psychologist, but this preference for an "ordinary" or "non-literary" way of earning his living should not be seen as implying any kind of division of his life into separate areas. In an interview with Gunnar Harding in 1973 he replied as follows to the question of how his writing relates to his work as a psychologist:

> I believe there is a very close connection, though it can't be seen. Everything one writes is an expression of a gathered experience. And the problems one meets in the world at large are present to a very great extent in what I write, though it doesn't always show directly. But it's close to hand, all the time.

Tranströmer is perhaps less in need of selection or pruning than many other poets, but even so the new reader will probably not want to plod through this volume straight from A to Z. Reading back from recent to early work could be more helpful than reading forward chronologically – an approach invited by the arrangement of May Swenson's selection (*Windows and Stones*, University of Pittsburgh Press, 1972). Whichever direction the new reader wants to follow, a few pointers may help.

17 Poems (1954) gathered pieces written by Tranströmer in his late teens and very early twenties and immediately announced the presence of a distinct poetic personality. The three longer pieces which conclude the collection suggest a kind of poetic ambition which the young Tranströmer soon lost – his notes on my first version of 'Elegy' for instance contain remarks like 'This poem was written by a romantic 22-year-old!' and 'Oh dear, how complicated I was in my younger days…' But the very first poem, suitably called

'Prelude', reveals a quality characteristic of all his writing, and that is the very sharply realised visual sense of his poems. The images leap out from the page, so the first-time reader or listener has the feeling of being given something very tangible, at once. In a way this quality seems to facilitate the translation – or rather the export-ation – of these poems, at least to the extent that sharply defined images may be "transposed" into another language. Poets like Pär Lagerkvist or Harry Martinson, much of whose work depends on very specific resonances of the Swedish language, are liable to lose much more in translation, and may indeed resist the process almost completely. Labouring over vowels and consonants may never have had much attraction for Tranströmer, but I think it is worth stress-ing for the foreign reader that in Tranströmer we are not dealing with any kind of "minimal" East European poet: he is very particular about the rhythm of his lines (sometimes the translator can find a parallel, sometimes he can't) and in the original Swedish his poems have an individual and unmistakable music of their own (I doubt if the translator can talk about "parallels" in any meaningful sense here).

'Prelude' also points forward thematically. It describes the process of waking up (note how this process appears not in the usual terms of rising to the surface but in terms of falling, of a parachute jump down into a vivid and teeming world). And this fascination with the borders between sleep and waking, with the strange areas of access between an everyday world we seem to know and another world we can't know in the same way but whose presence is undeniable – such a fascination has over the decades been one of Tranströmer's predominant themes. 'Dream Seminar', for example, from *The Wild Market-Square* (1983) deals directly with certain aspects of the relations between waking and dreaming states, but the reader will soon discover many poems which explore this region.

The way in which much or even most of Tranströmer's poetry describes, or allows for, or tries to come to terms with the powerful elements of our lives which we cannot consciously control or even satisfactorily define suggests, rightly, that there is a profoundly religious aspect to his response to the world and therefore in his poetry. In a largely secular country like Sweden such a writer may well be asked about religion in rather a blunt or naive manner (as if 'Do you believe in God?' were the same kind of question as 'Do you vote Social Democrat?') and Tranströmer has always replied to such questions cautiously. The following (from the Gunnar Harding interview already mentioned) is a characteristic response to the comment that reviewers sometimes refer to him as a mystic and sometimes as a religious poet:

Very pretentious words, mystic and so on. Naturally I feel reserved about
their use, but you could at least say that I respond to reality in such a
way that I look on existence as a great mystery and that at times, at
certain moments, this mystery carries a strong charge, so that it does
have a religious character, and it is often in such a context that I write.
So these poems are all the time pointing towards a greater context, one
that is incomprehensible to our normal everyday reason. Although it
begins in something very concrete

This movement towards a larger context is very important and it
reflects Tranströmer's distrust of over-simple formulations, slogans
and rhetorical gestures as short-cuts that can obscure and mislead.
It is in similar terms that we can see his response (or perhaps
refusal to respond directly) to the criticism of several reviewers of
the late 1960s and early 1970s that his poetry ignored current pol-
itical 'realities'. The assumption behind such criticism was that
poetry is just another element of political debate and its use of
language is no different from the leader-writer's use of language.
Many of his poems do deal with current 'realities', but with a care-
ful avoidance of the simplifications and aggressions of politicised
language and with an awareness of a wider and deeper context that
seemed beyond the range of the directly 'engaged' poetry of the
period, with its concern for taking 'positions' on a black-and-white
and rather parochial political map. See in particular 'About History'
from *Bells and Tracks* (1966), and then 'By the River', 'Outskirts',
'Traffic' and 'Night Duty' from *Seeing in the Dark* (1970).

To return to the religious aspects – the reader will notice how
specifically or overtly religious allusions in the early poetry soon
disappear from succeeding work. This has been interpreted as a
process of secularisation: I would rather see it as a way of trying to
do without the shorthand of everyday religious terminology in order
to try to define for oneself those areas in which a sense of imma-
nence may be experienced. We see something of this attempt in
poems like 'Secrets on the Way' and 'Tracks', both in Tranströmer's
1958 collection, where a series of contrasts, or similes, or just lum-
inously clear images, are grouped as if round a central space where
some kind of epiphany is or may be or has been experienced. Such
poems end by returning us, perhaps abruptly, to an active world, but
they leave us with the feeling that a strangeness has crossed our path.

Later forms of this development seem to entail two processes.
First, we can see some attempt to be more specific about this central
space or crossing-point, about this intrusion which can illuminate
or disturb our normal way of life: here we can find paradoxes,
imagery from and about dreams, speculations about how both past

and future can impinge upon the present, investigations into mem-
ory, and a fascination with the many ways in which borders, open
and closed, may be experienced. Second, we find a gradual move
away from the impersonality of the early poetry. Tranströmer can
still use the third person singular as a means of giving distance to
what is clearly first person singular experience – but from the late
1960s and the early 1970s we can watch an increasingly open in-
volvement of the poet's own personality as an element in the poems.
This is partly a matter of allowing more of the concrete starting-
point of the poem to appear in the poem (Tranströmer can name a
birth-place for nearly every poem), but it is also, more importantly,
a matter of letting himself appear in his poems as, in a sense, an
actor in his own dramas, both acting and being acted upon or
through. This process can be clearly followed in poems such as:
'Lament', in *The Half-Finished Heaven* (1962); 'Crests', 'Winter's
Formulae' and 'Alone', in *Bells and Tracks* (1966); 'Preludes',
'Upright' and 'The Bookcase' in *Seeing in the Dark* (1970); 'The
Outpost' and 'December 1972' in *Paths* (1973).

The lines of development I have roughly indicated reach a peak –
or perhaps a wave-crest may be more appropriate, for it is some-
thing in motion – in *Baltics* (1974), Tranströmer's longest poem to
date and one which marked a new expansiveness in his manner. Note
the plural of the title: here we have not one Baltic but a whole
series of them, reflecting the very different experience of those in
whose lives that particular sea has come to play a part; some of
these Baltics overlap, while some apparently contradict each other.
The poem seems to have been under way by about 1970 and two
external stimuli helped as starting-points. One was the finding of
a log-book kept by his (maternal) grandfather in the 1880s, listing
the ships he piloted (this is quoted from in Part One). The other
was his reading of Edward Lucie-Smith's English translation of
part of Jean Paul de Dadelsen's *Jonah*, which suggested to him a
manner or tone of voice for a long poem less monumental than the
accents of Eliot in *Four Quartets*. A third element should be men-
tioned and that is Tranströmer's lifelong interest in poems whose
growth parallels musical development: for instance, the three long
pieces which conclude *17 Poems* (and which were originally meant
to constitute one long poem) were intended to represent a parallel
to passacaglia form, and 'The Four Temperaments' in *Secrets on the
Way* aimed to echo Hindemith's *Theme and Variations: 'The Four
Temperaments'* for piano and string orchestra (1940). Reference to
specific musical works plays an important part in poems like
'Schubertiana' in *The Truth-Barrier* and the title poem of *The Sad*

Gondola. However much musical experience has undoubtedly inspired the poet, readers of the written text must decide for themselves in what sense *Baltics* fulfils Tranströmer's own claim that it is his 'most consistent attempt to write music'. At the very least, the pattern of thematic return and variation may recall similar patterns in many musical works. Tranströmer has further remarked that *Baltics* is in part a polemic against his earlier self, against the way in which his earlier poems from the Stockholm archipelago (the island of Runmarö has close family connections) treated the area as a protected oasis or reserve, whereas now *Baltics* treats the landscape and its life as open to the threats of the surrounding world.

The more relaxed manner of *Baltics* does not imply a more casual structure, however. It is not difficult for the reader new to the work to notice the arch-like patterning of themes, as outlined by the Danish critic Steen Andersen:

> Part Six, about the grandmother...is a parallel to Part One, about the grandfather; in both cases there is documentary knowledge about the family (photo, log-book) and in both cases the poet himself must enquire his way forward as regards other details of this past. From Part One, the sea, we are taken, in Part Two, to the land, but with many references to the life which Part One introduced and described to us; the churchyard stones seen by the I-figure unite past and present. In Part Three the I-figure is more present still, but here too mainly through observations of things left by the past (the font, a photo). Parts Four and Five describe immediate observations, as distinct from the family and historical memories we otherwise find in the book. And finally Part Six carries us back to the past (the grandmother) and to the present, especially in the closing lines...It is thus a matter of *people* in a particular *place*.

In its amplification of this outline, Kjell Espmark's account of *Baltics* lets us see the sequence as a climax in Tranströmer's work up to the early 1970s, and Espmark argues, rightly, that it is to its themes we must look to get to the heart of the poem. On the one hand we have distances, obstacles or frontiers; on the other we have attempts to overcome these, and even instances of spontaneous contact –

> The distance or blockage can change from one section to another – from historical and geographical distance to emotional isolation and the inability to articulate what 'wants to be said'. The bridging-over theme is modulated accordingly. The tension between the limiting and the uniting movements condenses in one point – a genuinely Tranströmerian oxymoron – 'the open frontier'. It is towards this epiphanously charged point that the movements of the poem strive.

In order to illustrate some of the foregoing, and also to give some idea of Tranströmer's own approach to his poems, it may be interesting to give a few examples from Tranströmer's own comments on his poems. He talks quite freely about his work and seems prepared to give his readers a great deal of freedom as to what they may find in his poems. Generally he is careful to avoid telling us what we ought to find:

The Journey's Formulae, first stanza (*Secrets on the Way*) [p.49]

Here is a man ploughing. It means something. Why have I now for half a year seen that man who is ploughing? No, it'll soon be a whole year. What does it mean? A month ago I finally understood what would happen. It's in Yugoslavia. At first I thought it was in a Swedish landscape in autumn – I was tricked by the lighting. No, it's Yugoslavia, in the middle of the day, and the sun is burning. It has something to do with the war. Or at least there are many dead people in the background – they move away later but what is really going on? It's no epic, it's a bagatelle, five lines perhaps. Yet terribly important to me... [Letter to Göran Palm, 1956]

In the Nile Delta (*The Half-Finished Heaven*) [p.62]

In the first place it is a direct description of something I actually experienced. It is not something I invented – I recount in the concentrated form of the poem the experiences of a day in the town of Tanta in Egypt in 1959. I and my wife (who was only nineteen then and had never before been confronted with the reality of a poor country) had with difficulty managed to escape from the tour guides – there was never any help available if it was a matter of making one's way into parts of the country which the authorities did not want to show to foreigners – and there we were in Tanta. It could be asked why I use 'he' instead of 'I' in the poem – I think it is a way of giving distance and generality to a difficult and troubling experience. I have tried to write as unsentimentally and nakedly as possible and mainly with monosyllabic words. Well – we went to sleep in the indescribably dirty ex-hotel and then I dreamt what is in the poem. The words which a 'voice' said were somewhat different – as often happens in dreams the words were nonsense-words, but they had the meaning I've given them in the poem. The dream helped me, it created a change of mood from negative feelings and hate towards something else – not to a "reconciliation" with the suffering around us but it gave a chance of seeing it without running away. If I were to philosophise about this I would say that I believe hate and rage are a first and natural reaction to the plight of poor countries but they don't give much inspiration to do anything about it. In the dream there was a strongly positive element, a sort of GOOD WILL. My immediate reaction to this experience was of a religious nature and a trace of this can be seen in for instance the third to last line, in the words alluding to the Gospel account of the sick people around the pool in Bethesda – it was when the water stirred that the pool had its miracle-working power. [John 5.2] [In reply to a question from Mats Dahlberg, 1968]

Night Duty (*Seeing in the Dark*) [p.92]

That bell-ringing at the end of 'Night Duty' – when I was walking around in the old Västerås churchyard, which was in the process of being dug up, and caught sight of that digging-machine's scoop, bell-ringing broke out from the Lutheran cathedral tower and it seemed to wrap the whole experience in something which each reader can interpret as he pleases, but which for me is in part something fatefully apocalyptic but also something like the sponge of religious faith which is reached down from above to swab one's face as one sits like a beaten boxer in the corner of the ring waiting for the next round (the last one?). [Letter to Göran Palm, 1970]

The Outpost (*Paths*) [p.100]

It began almost as a joke. It began very modestly. There was no intention it should become such a serious business, it was more something I passed the time with. The situation is this: I'm on a military exercise and get posted out to a heap of stones, a situation one experiences as quite absurd. And to cheer myself up a little I wrote the opening lines. I didn't mean any poem to come out of it. These first verses were written very easily just because I didn't have any feeling of 'now this is serious, you must achieve something'. But then gradually the poem came to deal with how I find myself in an absurd situation in life generally, as I often do. Life puts us in certain absurd situations and it's impossible to escape. And that's where the poem becomes very serious, in the fifth verse, which ends: 'I am the place / where creation is working itself out.' And that's a kind of religious idea which recurs here and there in my poems of late, that I see a kind of meaning in being present, in using reality, in experiencing it, in making something of it. And I have an inkling that I'm doing this as some sort of task or commission. It recurs further on in the book at the beginning of 'December Evening 1972' –

> Here I come, the invisible man, perhaps employed
> by a Great Memory to live right now...

It's a purely personal experience really, that I fulfil some function here, in the service of something else. This sounds pretentious and because of that the tone in such circumstances often becomes a little frivolous. [Conversation with Gunnar Harding, 1973]

Citoyens (*The Truth-Barrier*) [p.117]

It was in 1970, and I had an old Saab which had just been tested for roadworthiness. The verdict was that everything was in splendid order, including the brakes. Then when I was on the motorway, I found myself in a lane where everyone was driving fairly fast. Suddenly the cars in front of me slowed down. I stepped on the brakes but nothing happened. I drove right into the back of a Mercedes. My poor little car was like an accordeon. I survived. I stepped out. All I had was a shirt, a pair of trousers, shoes and a book about the French Revolution. That was all that was left after the accident. It was quite a shaking experience. I had a dream that night, and that is what I have recounted in the poem: I have not invented anything. Except perhaps the image of 'the plummet / that makes the clocks go...' [Conversation with Robert Bly, 1977]

The Gallery (*The Truth-Barrier*) [p.123]

'The Gallery' is the poem I've had on the go longest – it began some time ten years ago. It started with a particular experience. I had been out as a teacher on a course for social workers, in interview techniques. It was in Laxå. In the evening I go to the motel to sleep and then I have a sort of Judgement Day experience: what is it I'm really doing? I'm a psychologist, after all, so I ought to be an expert in interviewing people. Playing one's professional role comes easily, and in that role one is to a high degree protected. But now I seemed to be confronted with what it really was about. It was a very disturbing evening. I lay there and seemed to see how the pictures of a whole crowd of people I had met in my job unwound like a film, and suddenly I seemed to experience them as a human being, not just as a professional. The poem is quite simply a coming-to-terms with this professional role, even if I started writing it as a rhapsody on authentic life-stories. Yes, all those fates glimpsed in the poem are authentic, and I myself am there too, in the passage beginning 'An artist said...' There you find a self-portrait, which was actually written in quite another context but which I inserted here. I thought that I too belonged in the gallery.
[Conversation with Matts Rying, 1979]

17 POEMS
17 DIKTER
  (1954)

Prelude

Waking up is a parachute jump from dreams.
Free of the suffocating turbulence the traveller
sinks towards the green zone of morning.
Things flare up. From the viewpoint of the quivering lark
he is aware of the huge root-systems of the trees,
their swaying underground lamps. But above ground
there's greenery – a tropical flood of it – with
lifted arms, listening
to the beat of an invisible pump. And he
sinks towards summer, is lowered
in its dazzling crater, down
through shafts of green damp ages
trembling under the sun's turbine. Then it's checked,
this straight-down journey through the moment, and the wings spread
to the osprey's repose above rushing waters.
The bronze-age trumpet's
outlawed note
hovers above the bottomless depths.

In day's first hours consciousness can grasp the world
as the hand grips a sun-warmed stone.
The traveller is standing under the tree. After
the crash through death's turbulence, shall
a great light unfold above his head?

Autumnal Archipelago

Storm

Here the walker suddenly meets the giant
oak tree, like a petrified elk whose crown is
furlongs wide before the September ocean's
       murky green fortress.

Northern storm. The season when rowanberry
clusters swell. Awake in the darkness, listen:
constellations stamping inside their stalls, high
            over the tree-tops.

Evening – Morning

Moon – its mast is rotten, its sail is shrivelled.
Seagull – drunk and soaring away on currents.
Jetty – charred rectangular mass. The thickets
            founder in darkness.

Out on doorstep. Morning is beating, beats on
ocean's granite gateways and sun is sparkling
near the world. Half-smothered, the gods of summer
            fumble in sea-mist.

Ostinato

Under the buzzard's circling point of stillness
ocean rolls resoundingly on in daylight,
blindly chews its bridle of weed and snorts up
            foam over beaches.

Earth is veiled in darkness where bats can sense their
way. The buzzard stops and becomes a star now.
Ocean rolls resoundingly on and snorts up
            foam over beaches.

Five Stanzas to Thoreau

Yet one more abandoned the heavy city's
ring of greedy stones. And the water, salt and
crystal, closes over the heads of all who
            truly seek refuge.

Silence slowly spiralling up has risen
here from earth's recesses to put down roots and
grow and with its burgeoning crown to shade his
                    sun-heated doorstep.

                                *

Kicks a mushroom thoughtlessly. Thunder clouds are
piling on the skyline. Like copper trumpets
crooked roots of trees are resounding, foliage
                    scatters in terror.

Autumn's headlong flight is his weightless mantle,
flapping till again from the frost and ashes
peaceful days have come in their flocks and bathe their
                    claws in the well-spring.

                                *

Disbelief will meet him who saw a geyser
and escaped from wells filled with stones, like Thoreau
disappearing deep in his inner greenness
                    artful and hopeful.

Gogol

The jacket threadbare as a wolf-pack.
The face like a marble slab.
Sitting in the circle of his letters in the grove that rustles
with scorn and error,
the heart blowing like a scrap of paper through the inhospitable
passageways.

The sunset is now creeping like a fox over this country,
igniting the grass in a mere moment.
Space is full of horns and hooves and underneath
the barouche glides like a shadow between my father's
lit courtyards.

St Petersburg on the same latitude as annihilation
(did you see the beauty in the leaning tower)
and round the ice-bound tenements floating like a jellyfish
the poor man in his cloak.

And here, enveloped in fasts, is the man who before was surrounded by
         the herds of laughter,
but these have long since taken themselves to tracts far above the tree-line.
Men's unsteady tables.
Look outside, see how darkness burns hard a whole galaxy of souls.
Rise up then on your chariot of fire and leave the country!

Sailor's Yarn

There are bare winter days when the sea is kin
to mountain country, crouching in grey plumage,
a brief minute blue, long hours with waves like pale
lynxes vainly seeking hold in the beach-gravel.

On such a day wrecks might come from the sea searching
for their owners, settling in the town's din, and drowned
crews blow landward, thinner than pipe-smoke.

(The real lynxes are in the north, with sharpened claws
and dreaming eyes. In the north, where day
lives in a mine both day and night.

Where the sole survivor may sit
at the borealis stove and listen
to the music of those frozen to death.)

Strophe and Counter-Strophe

The outermost circle belongs to myth. There the helmsman sinks upright
among glittering fish-backs.
How far from us! When day
stands in a sultry windless unrest –
as the Congo's green shadow holds
the blue men in its vapour –
when all this driftwood on the heart's sluggish
coiling current
piles up.

Sudden change: in under the repose of the constellations
the tethered ones glide.
Stern high, in a hopeless
position, the hull of a dream, black
against the coastline's pink. Abandoned
the year's plunge, quick
and soundless – as the sledge-shadow, dog-like, big
travels over snow,
reaches the wood.

Agitated Meditation

A storm drives the mill sails wildly round
in the night's darkness, grinding nothing. – You
    are kept awake by the same laws.
The grey shark belly is your weak lamp.

Shapeless memories sink to the sea's depths
and harden there to strange columns. – Green
    with algae is your crutch. A man
who takes to the seas comes back stiffened.

The Stones

The stones we threw I hear
fall, glass-clear through the years. In the valley
the confused actions of the moment
fly screeching from
treetop to treetop, become silent
in thinner air than the present's, glide
like swallows from hilltop
to hilltop until they've
reached the furthest plateaux
along the frontier of being. There all
our deeds fall
glass-clear
with nowhere to fall to
except ourselves.

Context

Look at the grey tree. The sky has run
through its fibres down in the earth –
only a shrunk cloud is left when
the earth has drunk. Stolen space
is twisted in pleats, twined
to greenery. – The brief moments
of freedom rise in us, whirl
through the Parcae and further.

Morning Approach

The black-backed gull, the sun-captain, holds his course.
Beneath him is the water.
The world is still sleeping like a
multicoloured stone in the water.
Undeciphered day. Days –
like aztec hieroglyphs.

The music. And I stand trapped
in its Gobelin weave with
raised arms – like a figure
out of folk art.

There is Peace in the Surging Prow

On a winter morning you feel how this earth
plunges ahead. Against the house walls
an air-current smacks
out of hiding.

Surrounded by movement: the tent of calm.
And the secret helm in the migrating flock.
Out of the winter gloom
a tremolo rises

from hidden instruments. It is like standing
under summer's high lime tree with the din
of ten thousand
insect wings above your head.

Midnight Turning Point

The wood-ant watches silently, looks into
nothing. And nothing's heard but drips from dim
leafage and the night's murmuring deep in
    summer's canyon.

The spruce stands like the hand of a clock,
spiked. The ant glows in the hill's shadow.
Bird cry! And at last. The cloud-packs slowly
    begin to roll.

Song

The gathering of white birds grew: gulls
dressed in canvas from the sails of foundered ships
but stained by vapours from forbidden shores.

Alarm! Alarm! round refuse from a cargo boat.
They crowded in and formed an ensign-staff
that signalled 'Booty here'.

And gulls careered across watery wastes
with blue acres gliding in the foam.
Athwart, a phosphorescent pathway to the sun.

But Väinämöinen travels in his past
on oceans glittering in ancient light.
He rides. The horse's hooves are never wet.

Behind: the forest of his songs is green.
The oak whose leap's a thousand years long.
The mighty windmill turned by birdsong.

And every tree a prisoner in its soughing.
With giant cones glinting in the moonlight
when the distant pine glows like a beacon.

Then the Other rises with his spell
and the arrow, seeing far and wide, flees,
the feather singing like a flight of birds.

A dead second when the horse abruptly
stiffens, breaks across the waterline
like a blue cloud beneath the thunder's antenna.

And Väinämöinen plunges heavy in the sea
(a jumping-sheet the compass-points hold tight).
Alarm! Alarm! among the gulls around his fall!

Like one bewitched, without anxiety,
standing at the centre of the picture
of his joy, eleven corn-sheaves bulging.

Reliance – an alp-top humming in the ether
three thousand metres up where the clouds sail
races. The puffed basking shark wallows

guffawing soundlessly beneath the sea.
(Death and renewal when the wave arrives.)
And peacefully the breezes cycle through the leaves.

On the horizon thunder rumbles dully
(as the herd of buffalo flees in its dust).
The shadow of a fist clenches in the tree

and strikes down him who stands bewitched
in his joyous picture where the evening sky
seems to glow behind the wild-boar's mask of clouds.

His double, envious, arranges
a secret rendezvous with his woman.
And the shadow gathers and becomes a tidal wave

a tidal wave with riding seagulls darkened.
And the port-side heart sizzles in a breaker.
Death and renewal when the wave arrives.

The gathering of white birds grew: gulls
dressed in canvas from the sails of foundered ships
but stained by vapours from forbidden shores.

The herring-gull: a harpoon with a velvet back.
In close-up like a snowed-in hull
with hidden pulses glittering in rhythm.

His flier's nerves in balance. He soars.
Footless hanging in the wind he dreams
his hunter's dream with his beak's sharp shot.

He plunges to the surface, full-blossomed greed,
crams and jerks himself around his booty
as if he were a stocking. And then he rises like a spirit.

(Energies – their context is renewal,
more enigmatic than the eel's migrations.
A tree, invisible, in bloom. And as

the grey seal in its underwater sleep
rises to the surface, takes a breath
and dives – still asleep – to the seabed

so now the Sleeper in me secretly
has joined with *that* and has returned while I
stood staring fixedly at something else.)

And the diesel engine's throbbing in the flock
past the dark skerry, a cleft of birds
where hunger blossomed with stretched maw.

At night-fall they could still be heard:
an abortive music like that from
the orchestra pit before the play begins.

But on his ancient sea Väinämöinen drifted
shaken in the squall's mitt or supine
in the mirror-world of calms where the birds

were magnified. And from a stray seed, far
from land at the sea's edge growing
out of waves, out of a fogbank it sprang:

a mighty tree with scaly trunk, and leaves
quite transparent and behind them
the filled white sails of distant suns

glided on in trance. And now the eagle rises.

Elegy

At the outset. Like a fallen dragon
in some mist and vapour shrouded swamp,
our spruce-clad coastland lies. Far out there:
two steamers crying from a dream

in the fog. This is the lower world.
Motionless woods, motionless surface
and the orchid's hand that reaches from the soil.
On the other side, beyond these straits

but hanging in the same reflection: the Ship,
like the cloud hanging weightless in its space.
And the water round its prow is motionless,
becalmed. And yet – a storm is up!

and the steamer smoke blows level – the sun
flickers there in its grip – and the gale
is hard against the face of him who boards.
To make one's way up the port side of Death.

A sudden draught, the curtain flutters.
Silence ringing, an alarm clock.
A sudden draught, the curtain flutters.
Until a distant door is heard closing

far off in another year.

                    *

O field as grey as the buried bog-man's cloak.
And island floating darkly in the fog.
It's quiet, as when the radar turns
and turns its arc in hopelessness.

There's a crossroads in a moment.
Music of the distances converges.
All grown together in a leafy tree.
Vanished cities glitter in its branches.

From everywhere and nowhere a song
like crickets in the August dark. Embedded
like a wood-beetle, he sleeps here in the night,
the peat-bog's murdered traveller. The sap compels

his thoughts up to the stars. And deep
in the mountain: here's the cave of bats.
Here hang the years, the deeds, densely.
Here they sleep with folded wings.

One day they'll flutter out. A throng!
(From a distance, smoke from the cave mouth.)
But still their summer-winter sleep prevails.
A murmuring of distant waters. In the dark tree

a leaf that turns.

                    *

One summer morning a harrow catches
in dead bones and rags of clothing. – He
lay there after the peat-bog was drained
and now stands up and goes his way in light.

In every parish eddies golden seed
round ancient guilt. The armoured skull
in the ploughed field. A wanderer en route
and the mountain keeps an eye on him.

In every parish the marksman's tube is humming
at midnight when the wings unfold
and the past expands in its collapse
and darker than the heart's meteorite.

An absence of spirit makes the writing greedy.
A flag begins tò smack. The wings
unfold around the booty. This proud journey!
where the albatross ages to a cloud

in Time's jaws. And culture is a whaling-
station where the stranger walks
among white gables, playing children, and
still with each breath he takes he feels

the murdered giant's presence.

                          *

Soft black-cock crooning from the heavenly spheres.
The music, guiltless in our shadow, like
the fountain water rising among the wild beasts,
deftly petrified around the playing jets.

The bows disguised, a forest.
The bows like rigging in a torrent –
the cabin's smashed beneath the torrent's hooves –
within us, balanced like a gyroscope, is joy.

This evening the world's calm is reflected
when the bows rest on strings without being moved.
Motionless in mist the forest trees
and the water-tundra mirroring itself.

Music's voiceless half is here, like the scent
of resin round lightning-damaged spruce.
An underground summer for each of us.
There at the crossroads a shadow breaks free

and runs off to where the Bach trumpet points.
Sudden confidence, by grace. To leave behind
one's self-disguise here on this shore
where the wave breaks and slides away, breaks

and slides away.

Epilogue

December. Sweden is a beached
unrigged ship. Against the twilight sky
its masts are sharp. And twilight lasts
longer than day – the road here is stony:
not till midday does the light arrive
and winter's colosseum rise
lit by unreal clouds. At once
the white smoke rises, coiling from
the villages. The clouds are high on high.
The sea snuffles at the tree-of-heaven's roots
distracted, as if listening to something else.
(Over the dark side of the soul
there flies a bird, wakening
the sleepers with its cries. The refractor
turns, catches in another time,
and it is summer: mountains bellow, bulged
with light and the stream raises the sun's glitter
in transparent hand…All then gone
as when a film spills out of a projector.)

Now the evening star burns through the cloud.
Houses, trees and fences are enlarged, grow
in the soundless avalanche of darkness.
And beneath the star more and more develops
of the other, hidden landscape, that which lives
the life of contours on the night's X-ray.
A shadow pulls its sledge between the houses.
They are waiting.
                         Six o'clock – the wind
gallops thunderously along the village street,

in darkness, like a troop of horsemen. How
the black turmoil resounds and echoes!
The houses trapped in a dance of immobility,
the din like that of dreams. Gust upon gust
staggers over the bay away
to the open sea that tosses in the dark.
In space the stars signal desperately.
They're lit and quenched by headlong clouds
that only when they shade the light betray
their presence, like clouds of the past that go
scudding in the souls. When I walk past
the stable wall I hear in all that noise
the sick horse tramping inside.
And there's departure in the storm,
by a broken gate that bangs and bangs, a lamp
swaying from a hand, a beast that cackles
frightened on the hill. Departure in the thunderous
rumble over the byre roofs, the roaring
in the telephone wires, the shrill whistling
in the tiles on night's roof
and the tree tossing helplessly.

A wail of bagpipes is let loose! A wail
of bagpipes keeping step! Liberators.
A procession. A forest on the march!
A bow-wave seethes and darkness stirs,
and land and water move. And the dead,
gone under deck, they are with us,
with us on the way: a voyage, a journey
which is no wild rush but gives security.
And the world is always taking down its tent
anew. One summer day the wind takes hold
of the oak's rigging, hurls Earth forward.
The lily paddles with its hidden webbed foot
in the pond's embrace – the pond which is in flight.
A boulder rolls away in the halls of space.
In the summer twilight islands seem to rise
on the horizon. Old villages are on
their way, retreating further into woods
on the seasons' wheels with magpie-creaking.
When the year kicks off its boots, and the sun
climbs higher, the trees break out in leaves
and take the wind and sail out in freedom.

Below the mountain breaks the pinewood surf,
but summer's long warm groundswell comes,
flows through the treetops slowly, rests
a moment, sinks away again –
a leafless coast remains. And finally:
God's spirit, like the Nile: flooding
and sinking in a rhythm calculated
in texts from many epochs.

But He is also the immutable
and thus observed here seldom. It's from
the side He crosses the procession's path.

As when the steamer passes through the mist,
the mist that does not notice. Silence.
Faint glimmer of the lantern is the signal.

SECRETS ON THE WAY

HEMLIGHETER PÅ VÄGEN

(1958)

Solitary Swedish Houses

A mix-max of black spruce
and smoking moonbeams.
Here's the croft lying low
and not a sign of life.

Till the morning dew murmurs
and an old man opens
– with a shaky hand – his window
and lets out an owl.

Further off, the new building
stands steaming
with the laundry butterfly
fluttering at the corner

in the middle of a dying wood
where the mouldering reads
through spectacles of sap
the proceedings of the bark-drillers.

Summer with flaxen-haired rain
or one solitary thunder-cloud
above a barking dog.
The seed is kicking inside the earth.

Agitated voices, faces
fly in the telephone wires
on stunted rapid wings
across the moorland miles.

The house on an island in the river
brooding on its stony foundations.
Perpetual smoke – they're burning
the forest's secret papers.

The rain wheels in the sky.
The light coils in the river.
Houses on the slope supervise
the waterfall's white oxen.

Autumn with a gang of starlings
holding dawn in check.
The people move stiffly
in the lamplight's theatre.

Let them feel without alarm
the camouflaged wings
and God's energy
coiled up in the dark.

The Man who Awoke with Singing over the Roofs

Morning. May-rain. The city is still quiet
as a mountain hamlet. The streets quiet. And in
the sky a bluish-green aero-engine rumbles. –
            The window is open.

The dream where the sleeper is lying prostrate
turns transparent. He stirs, begins
groping for attention's instruments –
            almost in space.

Weather Picture

The October sea glistens coldly
with its dorsal fin of mirages.

Nothing is left that remembers
the white dizziness of yacht races.

An amber glow over the village.
And all sounds in slow flight.

A dog's barking is a hieroglyph
painted in the air above the garden

where the yellow fruit outwits
the tree and drops of its own accord.

The Four Temperaments

The probing eye turns the sun's rays into police batons.
And in the evening: the hubbub from a party in the flat below
sprouts up through the floor like unreal flowers.

Driving on the plain. Darkness. The coach seemed stuck on the spot.
An anti-bird screeched in starry emptiness.
The albino sun stood over tossing dark seas.

                         *

A man like an uprooted tree with croaking foliage
and lightning at attention saw the beast-smelling
sun rise up among pattering wings on the world's

rocky island surging ahead behind banners of foam through night
and day with white sea-birds howling
on the deck and all with a ticket to Chaos.

                         *

You need only close your eyes to hear plainly
the gulls' faint Sunday over the sea's endless parish.
A guitar begins twanging in the thicket and the cloud dawdles

slowly as the green sledge of late spring
– with the whinnying light in the shafts –
comes gliding on the ice.

                         *

Woke with my girl's heels clopping in the dream
and outside two snowdrifts like winter's abandoned gloves
while leaflets from the sun cascaded over the city.

The road never comes to an end. The horizon rushes ahead.
The birds shake in the tree. The dust whirls round the wheels.
All the rolling wheels that contradict death!

Caprichos

It's getting dark in Huelva: sooty palm-trees
and the train whistle's flurrying
silver-white bats.

The streets have been filled up with people.
And the woman hurrying in the throng cautiously weighs
the last daylight on the balance of her eyes.

The office windows are open. You can still hear
how the horse is tramping in there.
The old horse with the rubber-stamp hooves.

Not till midnight are the streets empty.
At last in all the offices: it's blue.

Up there in space:
trotting silently, sparkling and black,
unseen and unbound,
having thrown its rider:
a new constellation I call 'The Horse'.

Siesta

The stones' Whitsun. And with sparkling tongues . . .
The city without weight in the midday hours.
Burials in simmering light. The drum which drowns
locked-in eternity's pounding fists.

The eagle rises and rises over the sleepers.
Sleep where the mill-wheel turns like thunder.
Tramping from the horse with blindfolded eyes.
Locked-in eternity's pounding fists.

The sleepers hang like weights in the tyrants' clock.
The eagle drifts dead in the sun's streaming white current.
And echoing in time – as in Lazarus' coffin –
locked-in eternity's pounding fists.

Izmir at Three O'Clock

Just ahead in the almost empty street
two beggars, one without legs –
he's carried on the other one's back.

They stood – as on a midnight road an animal
stands blinded staring into the carlights –
for one moment before passing on

and scuttled across the street like boys
in a playground while the midday heat's
myriad of clocks ticked in space.

Blue flowed past on the waters, flickering.
Black crept and shrank, stared from stone.
White blew up to a storm in the eyes.

When three o'clock was tramped under hooves
and darkness pounded in the wall of light
the city lay crawling at the sea's door

gleaming in the vulture's telescopic sight.

Secrets on the Way

Daylight struck the face of a man who slept.
His dream was more vivid
but he did not awake.

Darkness struck the face of a man who walked
among the others in the sun's strong
impatient rays.

It was suddenly dark, like a downpour.
I stood in a room that contained every moment –
a butterfly museum.

And the sun still as strong as before.
Its impatient brushes were painting the world.

Tracks

2 a.m.: moonlight. The train has stopped
out in the middle of the plain. Far away, points of light in a town,
flickering coldly at the horizon.

As when someone has gone into a dream so deep
he'll never remember having been there
when he comes back to his room.

As when someone has gone into an illness so deep
everything his days were becomes a few flickering points, a swarm,
cold and tiny at the horizon.

The train is standing quite still.
2 a.m.: bright moonlight, few stars.

Kyrie

Sometimes my life opened its eyes in the dark.
A feeling as if crowds drew through the streets
in blindness and anxiety on the way towards a miracle,
while I invisibly remain standing.

As the child falls asleep in terror
listening to the heart's heavy tread.
Slowly, slowly until morning puts its rays in the locks
and the doors of darkness open.

A Man from Benin
*(on a photograph of a 15th century relief in bronze
from the Negro state of Benin, showing a Portuguese Jew)*

When darkness fell I was still
but my shadow pounded
against the drumskin of hopelessness.
When the pounding began to ease
I saw the image of an image
of a man coming forward
in the emptiness, a page
lying open.
Like going past a house
long since abandoned
and someone appears at the window.
A stranger. He was the navigator.

He seemed to take notice.
Came nearer without a step.
In a hat which moulded itself
imitating our hemisphere
with the brim at the equator.
The hair parted in two fins.
The beard hung curled
round his mouth like eloquence.
He held his right arm bent.
It was thin like a child's.
The falcon that should have had its place
on his arm grew out
from his features.
He was the ambassador.
Interrupted in the middle of a speech
which the silence continues
even more forcibly.
Three peoples were silent in him.
He was the image of three peoples.
A Jew from Portugal,
who sailed away with the others,
the drifting and the waiting ones,
the hunched up flock
in the caravelle which was
their rocking wooden mother.
Landfall in a strange air
which made the atmosphere furry.
Observed in the market-place
by the negro cast-maker.
Long in his eyes' quarantine.
Reborn in the race of metal:
'I am come to meet him
who raises his lantern
to see himself in me.'

Balakirev's Dream
(1905)

The black grand piano, the gleaming spider
trembled at the centre of its net of music.

In the concert hall a land was conjured up
where stones were no heavier than dew.

But Balakirev dozed off during the music
and dreamed a dream about the tsar's droshky.

It rumbled over the cobblestones
straight into the crow-cawing blackness.

He sat alone inside the cab and looked
and also ran alongside on the road.

He knew the journey had lasted long
and his watch showed years, not hours.

There was a field where the plough lay
and the plough was a fallen bird.

There was an inlet where the vessel lay
ice-bound, lights out, with people on deck.

The droshky glided there across the ice
and the wheels spun with a sound of silk.

A lesser battleship: 'Sebastopol.'
He was aboard. The crew gathered round.

'You won't die if you can play.'
They showed a curious instrument.

Like a tuba, or a phonograph,
or a part of some unknown machine.

Stiff with fear and helpless he knew: it is
the instrument that drives the man-of-war.

He turned towards the nearest sailor,
made signs despairingly and begged:

'Cross yourself, like me, cross yourself!'
The sailor stared sadly like a blind man,

stretched out his arms, sank his head –
he hung as if nailed in the air.

The drums beat. The drums beat. Applause!
Balakirev wakened from his dream.

The wings of applause pattered in the hall.
He saw the man at the grand piano rise.

Outside the streets lay darkened by the strike.
The droshkies were rushing through the dark.

After an Attack

The sick boy.
Locked in a vision
with his tongue stiff as a horn.

He sits with his back turned to the picture of the cornfield.
The bandage round his jaw hinting at embalming.
His glasses are thick like a diver's. And everything is unanswered
and vehement like the telephone ringing in the dark.

But the picture behind him – a landscape that gives peace though the
          grain is a golden storm.
Sky like blue-weed and drifting clouds. Beneath in the yellow surge
some white shirts are sailing: reapers – they cast no shadows.

There's a man standing far across the field and he seems to be looking
        this way.
A broad hat darkens his face.
He seems to be observing the dark figure here in the room, perhaps
        to help.
Imperceptibly the picture has begun widening and opening behind the
        sick brooding
invalid. It sparks and pounds. Every grain is ablaze to rouse him!
The other – in the corn – gives a sign.

He has come close.
No one notices.

The Journey's Formulae
(from the Balkans, 1955)

1

A murmur of voices behind the ploughman.
He doesn't look round. The empty fields.
A murmur of voices behind the ploughman.
One by one the shadows break loose
and plunge into the summer sky's abyss.

2

Four oxen come, under the sky.
Nothing proud about them. And the dust thick
as wool. The insects' pens scrape.

A swirl of horses, lean as in
grey allegories of the plague.
Nothing gentle about them. And the sun raves.

3

The stable-smelling village with thin dogs.
The party official in the market square
in the stable-smelling village with white houses.

His heaven accompanies him: it is high
and narrow like inside a minaret.
The wing-trailing village on the hillside.

4

An old house has shot itself in the forehead.
Two boys kick a ball in the twilight.
A swarm of rapid echoes. – Suddenly, starlight.

5

On the road in the long darkness. My wristwatch
gleams obstinately with time's imprisoned insect.

The quiet in the crowded compartment is dense.
In the darkness the meadows stream past.

But the writer is halfway into his image, there
he travels, at the same time eagle and mole.

THE HALF-FINISHED HEAVEN
DEN HALVFÄRDIGA HIMLEN
(1962)

The Couple

They switch off the light and its white shade
glimmers for a moment before dissolving
like a tablet in a glass of darkness. Then up.
The hotel walls rise into the black sky.

The movements of love have settled, and they sleep
but their most secret thoughts meet as when
two colours meet and flow into each other
on the wet paper of a schoolboy's painting.

It is dark and silent. But the town has pulled closer
tonight. With quenched windows. The houses have approached.
They stand close up in a throng, waiting,
a crowd whose faces have no expressions.

The Tree and the Sky

There's a tree walking around in the rain,
it rushes past us in the pouring grey.
It has an errand. It gathers life
out of the rain like a blackbird in an orchard.

When the rain stops so does the tree.
There it is, quiet on clear nights
waiting as we do for the moment
when the snowflakes blossom in space.

Face to Face

In February living stood still.
The birds flew unwillingly and the soul
chafed against the landscape as a boat
chafes against the pier it lies moored to.

The trees stood with their backs turned towards me.
The deep snow was measured with dead straws.
The footprints grew old out on the crust.
Under a tarpaulin language pined.

One day something came to the window.
Work was dropped, I looked up.
The colours flared. Everything turned round.
The earth and I sprang towards each other.

Ringing

And the thrush blew its song on the bones of the dead.
We stood under a tree and felt time sinking and sinking.
The churchyard and the schoolyard met and widened into each other
      like two streams in the sea.

The ringing of the churchbells rose to the four winds borne by the
      gentle leverage of gliders.
It left behind a mightier silence on earth
and a tree's calm steps, a tree's calm steps.

Through the Wood

A place called Jacob's marsh
is the summer day's cellar
where the light sours to a drink
tasting of old age and slums.

The feeble giants stand entangled
closely – so nothing can fall.
The cracked birch moulders there
in an upright position like a dogma.

From the bottom of the wood I rise.
It grows light between the trunks.
It is raining over my roofs.
I am a water-spout for impressions.

At the edge of the wood the air is warm.
Great spruce, turned away and dark
whose muzzle hidden in the earth's mould
drinks the shadow of a shower.

November with Nuances of Noble Fur

It is the sky's being so grey
that makes the ground begin to shine:
the meadows with their timid green,
the ploughed fields dark as black-bread.

There is the red wall of a barn.
And there are acres under water
like shining rice-paddies in an Asia –
the gulls stand there reminiscing.

Misty spaces deep in the woods
chiming softly against each other.
Inspiration that lives secluded
and flees among the trees like Nils Dacke.

The Journey

In the underground station.
A crowding among placards
in a staring dead light.

The train came and collected
faces and portfolios.

Darkness next. We sat
in the carriages like statues,
hauled through the caverns.
Restraint, dreams, restraint.

In stations under sea-level
they sold the news of the dark.
People in motion sadly
silently under the clock-dials.

The train carried
outer garments and souls.

Glances in all directions
on the journey through the mountain.
Still no change.

But nearer the surface a murmuring
of bees began – freedom.
We stepped out of the earth.

The land beat its wings
once and became still
under us, widespread and green.

Ears of corn blew in
over the platforms.

Terminus – I
followed on, further.

How many were with me? Four,
five, hardly more.

Houses, roads, skies,
blue inlets, mountains
opened their windows.

C Major

When he came down to the street after the rendezvous
the air was swirling with snow.
Winter had come
while they lay together.
The night shone white.
He walked quickly with joy.
The whole town was downhill.
The smiles passing by –
everyone was smiling behind turned-up collars.
It was free!
And all the question-marks began singing of God's being.
So he thought.

A music broke out
and walked in the swirling snow
with long steps.
Everything on the way towards the note C.
A trembling compass directed at C.
One hour higher than the torments.
It was easy!
Behind turned-up collars everyone was smiling.

Noon Thaw

The morning air delivered its letters with stamps which glowed.
The snow shone and all burdens lightened – a kilo weighed just 700
      grammes.

The sun was high over the ice hovering on the spot both warm and cold.
The wind came out gently as if it were pushing a pram.

Families came out, they saw open sky for the first time in ages.
We found ourselves in the first chapter of a very gripping story.

The sunshine stuck to all the fur caps like pollen on bees
and the sunshine stuck to the name WINTER and stayed there till winter
      was over.

A still-life of logs on the snow made me thoughtful. I asked them:
'Are you coming along to my childhood?' They answered 'Yes.'

In among the copses there was a murmuring of words in a new language:
the vowels were blue sky and the consonants were black twigs and the
      speech was soft over the snow.

But the jet plane curtsying in its skirts of noise
made the silence on earth even stronger.

When We Saw the Islands Again

As the boat out there draws near
a sudden downpour makes it blind.
Quicksilver shot bounces on the water.
The blue-grey lies down.

The sea's there in the cottages too.
A stream of light in the dark hallway.
Heavy steps upstairs
and chests with newly-ironed smiles.
An Indian orchestra of copper pans.
A baby with eyes all at sea.

(The rain starts disappearing.
The smoke takes a few faltering steps
in the air above the roofs.)

Here comes more
bigger than dreams.

The beach with the hovels of elms.
A notice with the word CABLE.
The old heathery moor shines
for someone who comes flying.

Behind the rocks rich furrows
and the scarecrow our outpost
beckoning the colours to itself.

An always bright surprise
when the island reaches out a hand
and pulls me up from sadness.

From the Mountain

I stand on the mountain and look across the bay.
The boats rest on the surface of summer.
'We are sleepwalkers. Moons adrift.'
So say the white sails.

'We slip through a sleeping house.
We gently open the doors.
We lean towards freedom.'
So say the white sails.

Once I saw the wills of the world sailing.
They held the same course – one single fleet.
'We are dispersed now. No one's escort.'
So say the white sails.

Espresso

The black coffee they serve out of doors
among tables and chairs gaudy as insects.

Precious distillations
filled with the same strength as Yes and No.

It's carried out from the gloomy kitchen
and looks into the sun without blinking.

In the daylight a dot of beneficent black
that quickly flows into a pale customer.

It's like the drops of black profoundness
sometimes gathered up by the soul,

giving a salutary push: Go!
Inspiration to open your eyes.

The Palace

We stepped in. A single vast hall,
silent and empty, where the surface of the floor lay
like an abandoned skating rink.
All doors shut. The air grey.

Paintings on the walls. We saw
pictures throng lifelessly: shields, scale-
pans, fishes, struggling figures
in a deaf and dumb world on the other side.

A sculpture was set out in the void:
in the middle of the hall alone a horse stood
but at first when we were absorbed
by all the emptiness we did not notice him.

Fainter than the breathing in a shell
sounds and voices from the town
circling in this desolate space
murmuring and seeking power.

Also something else. Something darkly
set itself at our senses' five
thresholds without stepping over them.
Sand ran in every silent glass.

It was time to move. We walked
over to the horse. It was gigantic,
dark as iron. An image of power itself
abandoned when the princes left.

The horse spoke: 'I am The Only One.
The emptiness that rode me I have thrown.
This is my stable. I am growing quietly.
And I eat the silence that's in here.'

Syros

In Syros harbour left-over cargo steamers lay waiting.
Prow by prow by prow. Moored many years since:
CAPE RION, Monrovia.
KRITOS, Andros.
SCOTIA, Panama.

Dark pictures on the water, they have been hung away.

Like toys from our childhood which have grown to giants
and accuse us
of what we never became.

XELATROS, Pireus.
CASSIOPEIA, Monrovia.
The sea has read them through.

But the first time we came to Syros, it was at night,
we saw prow by prow by prow in the moonlight and thought:
what a mighty fleet, magnificent connections.

In the Nile Delta

The young wife wept over her food
in the hotel after a day in the city
where she saw the sick creep and huddle
and children bound to die of want.

She and her husband went to their room.
Sprinkled water to settle the dirt.
Lay on their separate beds with few words.
She fell in a deep sleep. He lay awake.

Out in the darkness a great noise ran past.
Murmurs, tramping, cries, carts, songs.
All in want. Never came to a stop.
And he sank in sleep curled in a No.

A dream came. He was on a voyage.
In the grey water a movement swirled
and a voice said: 'There is one who is good.
There is one who can see all without hating.'

A Dark Swimming Figure

About a prehistoric painting
on a rock in the Sahara:
a dark swimming figure
in an old river which is young.

Without weapons or strategy,
neither at rest nor quick
and cut from his own shadow
gliding on the bed of the stream.

He struggled to make himself free
from a slumbering green picture,
to come at last to the shore
and be one with his own shadow.

Lament

He laid aside his pen.
It rests still on the table.
It rests still in the empty room.
He laid aside his pen.

Too much that can neither be written nor kept silent!
He is paralysed by something happening far away
although the wonderful travelling-bag throbs like a heart.

Outside it is early summer.
From the greenery come whistlings – men or birds?
And cherry trees in bloom embrace the lorries which have come home.

Weeks go by.
Night comes slowly.
The moths settle on the window pane:
small pale telegrams from the world.

Allegro

I play Haydn after a black day
and feel a simple warmth in my hands.

The keys are willing. Soft hammers strike.
The resonance green, lively and calm.

The music says freedom exists
and someone doesn't pay the emperor tax.

I push down my hands in my Haydnpockets
and imitate a person looking on the world calmly.

I hoist the Haydnflag – it signifies:
'We don't give in. But want peace.'

The music is a glass-house on the slope
where the stones fly, the stones roll.

And the stones roll right through
but each pane stays whole.

The Half-Finished Heaven

Despondency breaks off its course.
Anguish breaks off its course.
The vulture breaks off its flight.

The eager light streams out,
even the ghosts take a draught.

And our paintings see daylight,
our red beasts of the ice-age studios.

Everything begins to look around.
We walk in the sun in hundreds.

Each man is a half-open door
leading to a room for everyone.

The endless ground under us.

The water is shining among the trees.

The lake is a window into the earth.

Nocturne

I drive through a village at night, the houses rise up
in the glare of my headlights – they're awake, want to drink.
Houses, barns, signs, abandoned vehicles – it's now
they clothe themselves in Life. – The people are sleeping:

some can sleep peacefully, others have drawn features
as if training hard for eternity.
They don't dare let go though their sleep is heavy.
They rest like lowered crossing-barriers when the mystery draws past.

Outside the village the road goes far among the forest trees.
And the trees the trees keeping silence in concord with each other.
They have a theatrical colour, like firelight.
How distinct each leaf! They follow me right home.

I lie down to sleep, I see strange pictures
and signs scribbling themselves behind my eyelids
on the wall of the dark. Into the slit between wakefulness and dream
a large letter tries to push itself in vain.

A Winter Night

The storm puts its mouth to the house
    and blows to produce a note.
I sleep uneasily, turn, with shut eyes
    read the storm's text.

But the child's eyes are large in the dark
    and for the child the storm howls.
Both are fond of lamps that swing.
    Both are halfway towards speech.

The storm has childish hands and wings.
    The Caravan bolts towards Lapland.
And the house feels its own constellation of nails
    holding the walls together.

The night is calm over our floor
    (where all expired footsteps
rest like sunk leaves in a pond)
    but outside the night is wild.

Over the world goes a graver storm.
    It sets its mouth to our soul
And blows to produce a note. We dread
    that the storm will blow us empty.

BELLS AND TRACKS

KLANGER OCH SPÅR

(1966)

Portrait with Commentary

Here is a portrait of a man I knew.
He's sitting at the table, his newspaper open.
The eyes settle down behind the glasses.
The suit is washed with the shimmer of pinewoods.

It's a pale and half-complete face. –
Yet he always inspired trust. Which is why
people would hesitate to come near him
for fear of meeting some misfortune.

His father earned money like dew.
But no one felt secure there at home –
always a feeling that alien thoughts
broke into the house at night.

The newspaper, that big dirty butterfly,
the chair and the table and the face are at rest.
Life has stopped in big crystals.
But may it stop there only till further notice!

                    *

That which is I in him is at rest.
It exists. He doesn't notice
and therefore it lives, exists.

What am I? Now and then long ago
I came for a few seconds quite close
to ME, to ME, to ME.

But the moment I caught sight of ME
I lost ME – there was only a hole
through which I fell like Alice.

Lisbon

In the Alfama quarter the yellow tramcars sang on the steep slopes.
There were two prisons. One was for thieves.
They waved through the grilled windows.
They shouted that they wanted to be photographed.

'But here,' said the conductor giggling like a split man
'here sit politicians.' I saw the façade the façade the façade
and high up in a window a man
who stood with a telescope to his eye and looked out over the sea.

Laundry hung in blue air. The walls were hot.
The flies read microscopic letters.
Six years later I asked a woman from Lisbon:
'Is it true, or have I dreamt it?'

From an African Diary
(1963)

On the Congolese market-place pictures
shapes move thin as insects, deprived of their human power.
It's a hard passage between two ways of life.
He who has arrived has a long way to go.

A young man found a foreigner lost among the huts.
Didn't know whether to take him for a friend or a subject for extortion.
His doubt disturbed him. They parted in confusion.

The Europeans mostly stay clustered round the car as if it were Mamma.
The crickets are as strong as electric shavers. The car drives home.
Soon the beautiful darkness comes, taking charge of the dirty clothes.
        Sleep.
He who has arrived has a long way to go.

It helps perhaps with hand-shakes like a flight of migratory birds.
It helps perhaps to let the truth out of the books.
It is necessary to go further.

The student reads in the night, reads and reads to be free
and having passed his exam he becomes a step for the next man.
A hard passage.
He who has gone furthest has a long way to go.

Crests

With a sigh the lifts begin to rise
in high blocks delicate as porcelain.
It will be a hot day out on the asphalt.
The traffic signs have drooping eyelids.

The land a steep slope to the sky.
Crest after crest, no proper shadow.
We fly there on the hunt for You
through the summer in cinemascope.

And in the evening I lie like a ship
with lights out, just at the right distance
from reality, while the crew
swarm in the parks there ashore.

Hommages

Walked along the antipoetic wall.
Die Mauer. Don't look over.
It wants to surround our adult lives
in the routine city, the routine landscape.

Éluard touched some button
and the wall opened
and the garden showed itself.

I used to go with the milk pail through the wood.
Purple trunks on all sides.
An old joke hung in there
as beautiful as a votive ship.

Summer read out of *Pickwick Papers*.
The good life, a tranquil carriage
crowded with excited gentlemen.

Close your eyes, change horses.

In distress come childish thoughts.
We sat by the sickbed and prayed
for a pause in the terror, a breach
where the Pickwicks could pull in.

Close your eyes, change horses.

It is easy to love fragments
that have been on the way a long time.
Inscriptions on church bells
and proverbs written across saints
and many-thousand-year-old seeds.

Archilochos! – No answer.

The birds roamed over the seas' rough pelt.
We locked ourselves in with Simenon
and felt the smell of human life
where the serials debouch.

Feel the smell of truth.

The open window has stopped
in front of the treetops here
and the evening sky's farewell letter.

Shiki, Björling and Ungaretti
with life's chalks on death's blackboard.
The poem which is completely possible.

I looked up when the branches swung.
White gulls were eating black cherries.

Winter's Formulae

1

I fell asleep in my bed
and woke up under the keel.

At four o'clock in the morning
when life's clean picked bones
coldly associate with each other.

I fell asleep among the swallows
and woke up among the eagles.

2

In the lamplight the ice on the road
is gleaming like lard.

This is not Africa.
This is not Europe.
This is nowhere other than 'here'.

And that which was 'I'
is only a word
in the December dark's mouth.

3

The institute's pavilions
displayed in the dark
shine like TV screens.

A hidden tuning-fork
in the great cold
sends out its tone.

I stand under the starry sky
and feel the world creep
in and out of my coat
as in an ant-hill.

4

Three dark oaks sticking out of the snow.
So gross, but nimble-fingered.
Out of their giant bottles
the greenery will bubble in spring.

5

The bus crawls through the winter evening.
It glimmers like a ship in the spruce forest
where the road is a narrow deep dead canal.

Few passengers: some old and some very young.
If it stopped and quenched the lights
the world would be deleted.

Morning Birds

I waken the car
whose windscreen is coated with pollen.
I put on my sunglasses.
The birdsong darkens.

Meanwhile another man buys a paper
at the railway station
close to a large goods wagon
which is all red with rust
and stands flickering in the sun.

No blank space anywhere here.

Straight through the spring warmth a cold corridor
where someone comes running
and tells how up at head office
they slandered him.

Through a back door in the landscape
comes the magpie
black and white.
And the blackbird darting to and fro
till everything becomes a charcoal drawing,
except the white clothes on the washing-line:
a palestrina chorus.

No blank space anywhere here.

Fantastic to feel how my poem grows
while I myself shrink.
It grows, it takes my place.
It pushes me aside.
It throws me out of the nest.
The poem is ready.

About History

1

One day in March I go down to the sea and listen.
The ice is as blue as the sky. It is breaking up under the sun.
The sun which also whispers in a microphone under the covering of
        ice.
It gurgles and froths. And someone seems to be shaking a sheet far
        out.
It's all like History: our Now. We are submerged, we listen.

2

Conferences like flying islands about to crash . . .
Then: a long trembling bridge of compromises.
There shall the whole traffic go, under the stars,
under the unborn pale faces,
outcast in the vacant spaces, anonymous as grains of rice.

3

Goethe travelled in Africa in '26 disguised as Gide and saw everything.
Some faces become clearer from everything they see after death.
When the daily news from Algeria was read out
there appeared a large house where all the windows were blacked,
all except one. And there we saw the face of Dreyfus.

4

Radical and Reactionary live together as in an unhappy marriage,
moulded by one another, dependent on one another.
But we who are their children must break loose.
Every problem cries in its own language.
Go like a bloodhound where the truth has trampled.

5

Out on the open ground not far from the buildings
an abandoned newspaper has lain for months, full of events.
It grows old through nights and days in rain and sun,
on the way to becoming a plant, a cabbage-head, on the way to being
        united with the earth.
Just as a memory is slowly transmuted into your own self.

Alone

I

One evening in February I came near to dying here.
The car skidded sideways on the ice, out
on the wrong side of the road. The approaching cars –
their lights – closed in.

My name, my girls, my job
broke free and were left silently behind
further and further away. I was anonymous
like a boy in a playground surrounded by enemies.

The approaching traffic had huge lights.
They shone on me while I pulled at the wheel
in a transparent terror that floated like egg white.
The seconds grew – there was space in them –
they grew as big as hospital buildings.

You could almost pause
and breathe out for a while
before being crushed.

Then something caught: a helping grain of sand
or a wonderful gust of wind. The car broke free
and scuttled smartly right over the road.
A post shot up and cracked – a sharp clang – it
flew away in the darkness.

Then – stillness. I sat back in my seat-belt
and saw someone coming through the whirling snow
to see what had become of me.

II

I have been walking for a long time
on the frozen Östergötland fields.
I have not seen a single person.

In other parts of the world
there are people who are born, live and die
in a perpetual crowd.

To be always visible – to live
in a swarm of eyes –
a special expression must develop.
Face coated with clay.

The murmuring rises and falls
while they divide up among themselves
the sky, the shadows, the sand grains.

I must be alone
ten minutes in the morning
and ten minutes in the evening.
– Without a programme.

Everyone is queuing at everyone's door.

Many.

One.

On the Outskirts of Work

In the middle of work
we start longing fiercely for wild greenery,
for the Wilderness itself, penetrated only
by the thin civilisation of the telephone wires.

                    *

The moon of leisure circles the planet Work
with its mass and weight. – That's how they want it.
When we are on the way home the ground pricks up its ears.
The underground listens to us via the grass-blades.

                    *

Even in this working day there is a private calm.
As in a smoky inland area where a canal flows:
THE BOAT appears unexpectedly in the traffic
or glides out behind the factory, a white vagabond.

                    *

One Sunday I walk past an unpainted new building
standing before a grey wet surface.
It is half finished. The wood has the same light colour
as the skin on someone bathing.

*

Outside the lamps the September night is totally dark.
When the eyes adjust, there is faint light
over the ground where large snails glide out
and the mushrooms are as numerous as the stars.

After Someone's Death

Once there was a shock
which left behind a long pale glimmering comet's tail.
It contains us. It makes TV pictures blurred.
It deposits itself as cold drops on the aerials.

You can still shuffle along on skis in the winter sun
among groves where last year's leaves still hang.
They are like pages torn from old telephone directories –
the subscribers' names are eaten up by the cold.

It is still beautiful to feel your heart throbbing.
But often the shadow feels more real than the body.
The samurai looks insignificant
beside his armour of black dragon-scales.

Oklahoma

1

The train stopped far south. There was snow in New York.
Here you could go about in shirtsleeves the whole night.
But no one was out. Only the cars
flew past in their glare, flying saucers.

2

'We battlefields who are proud
of our many dead . . .'
said a voice while I wakened.

The man behind the counter said:
'I'm not trying to sell it,
I'm not trying to sell it,
I only want you to look at it.'
And he showed the Indians' axes.

The boy said:
'I know I have a prejudice,
I don't want to be left with it sir.
What do you think of us?'

3

This motel is a strange shell. With a hired car
(a huge white servant outside the door)
almost without memory and without ploy
at last I can settle on my point of balance.

Summer Plain

We have seen so much.
Reality has used us up so much,
but here is summer at last:

a large airfield – the flight controller is bringing down
load after load of frozen
people from space.

The grass and the flowers – here we land.
The grass has a green manager.
I report myself.

Downpour over the Interior

The rain is hammering on the car roofs.
The thunder rumbles. The traffic slows down.
The lights are switched on in the middle of the summer day.

The smoke pours down the chimneys.
All living things huddle, shut their eyes.
A movement inwards, feel life stronger.

The car is almost blind. He stops
lights a private fire and smokes
while the water swills along the windows.

Here on a forest road, winding and out of the way
near a lake with water lilies
and a long mountain that vanishes in the rain.

Up there lie the piles of stones
from the iron age when this was a place
for tribal wars, a colder Congo

and the danger drove beasts and men together
to a murmuring refuge behind the walls,
behind thickets and stones on the hilltop.

A dark slope, someone moving
up clumsily with his shield on his back
– this he imagines while his car is standing.

It begins to lighten, he winds down the window.
A bird flutes away to itself
in a thinning silent rain.

The lake surface is taut. The thunder-sky whispers
down through the water lilies to the mud.
The forest windows are slowly opening.

But the thunder strikes out of the stillness!
A deafening clap. And then a void
where the last drops fall.

In the silence he hears an answer coming.
From far away. A kind of coarse child's voice.
It rises, a bellowing from the hill.

A roar of mingled notes.
A long-hoarse trumpet from the iron age.
Perhaps from inside himself.

Under Pressure

The blue sky's engine-drone is deafening.
We're living here on a shuddering work-site
where the ocean depths can suddenly open up –
shells and telephones hiss.

You can see beauty only from the side, hastily.
The dense grain on the field, many colours in a yellow stream.
The restless shadows in my head are drawn there.
They want to creep into the grain and turn to gold.

Darkness falls. At midnight I go to bed.
The smaller boat puts out from the larger boat.
You are alone on the water.
Society's dark hull drifts further and further away.

Open and Closed Spaces

A man feels the world with his work like a glove.
He rests for a while at midday having laid aside the gloves on the shelf.
There they suddenly grow, spread
and black-out the whole house from inside.

The blacked-out house is away out among the winds of spring.
'Amnesty,' runs the whisper in the grass: 'amnesty.'
A boy sprints with an invisible line slanting up in the sky
where his wild dream of the future flies like a kite bigger than the
          suburb.

Further north you can see from a summit the blue endless carpet of
          pine forest
where the cloud shadows
are standing still.
No, are flying.

An Artist in the North

I Edvard Grieg moved like a free man among men.
Ready with a joke, read the papers, travelled here and there.
Led the orchestra.
The concert-hall with its lamps trembling in triumph like the train-ferry
          when it puts in.

I have brought myself up here to be shut in with silence.
My work-cottage is small.
The piano a tight fit like the swallow under the eaves.

For the most part the beautiful steep slopes say nothing.
There is no passageway
but sometimes a little hatch opens
and a strangely seeping light direct from trolldom.

Reduce!

And the hammer-blows in the mountain came
came
came
came one spring night into our room
disguised as beating of the heart.

The year before I die I'll send out four hymns to track down God.
But it starts here.
A song about what is near.

What is near.

The battlefield within us
where we the Bones of the Dead
fight to become living.

In the Open

1

Late autumn labyrinth.
At the entrance to the wood a discarded empty bottle.
Go in. At this season the woods are silently deserted halls.
Only a few kinds of noise: as if someone were removing twigs cautiously
          with tweezers
or a hinge creaking faintly inside a thick tree trunk.
The frost has breathed on the mushrooms and they have shrivelled.
They are like objects and garments found after a disappearance.
Now twilight comes. It's a matter of getting out
and seeing your landmarks again: the rusty implement out on the field
and the house on the other side of the lake, a russet square strong
          as a bouillon cube.

2

A letter from America set me off, drove me out
one light night in June on the empty streets in the suburb
among newborn blocks without memory, cool as blueprints.

The letter in my pocket. Desperate furious striding, it is a kind of
        pleading.
With you, evil and good really have faces.
With us, it's mostly a struggle between roots, ciphers and shades of
        light.

Those who run death's errands don't avoid the daylight.
They rule from glass storeys. They swarm in the sun's blaze.
They lean across the counter and turn their heads.

Far away I happen to stop before one of the new façades.
Many windows all merging together into one single window.
The light of the night sky is caught there and the gliding of the
                treetops .
It is a mirroring sea without waves, erect in the summer night.

Violence seems unreal
for a little.

3

The sun scorches. The plane flies low
throwing a shadow in the form of a large cross rushing forward on the
        ground.
A man is crouching in the field at something.
The shadow comes.
For a fraction of a second he is in the middle of the cross.

I have seen the cross that hangs under cool church vaults.
Sometimes it's like a snapshot
of something in violent movement.

Slow Music

The building is closed. The sun crowds in through the windows
and warms up the surfaces of desks
that are strong enough to take the load of human fate.

We are outside, today, on the long wide slope.
Many have dark clothes. You can stand in the sun with your eyes shut
and feel yourself being slowly blown forward.

I come down to the water too seldom. But here I am now,
among large stones with peaceful backs.
Stones which slowly migrated backwards up out of the waves.

SEEING IN THE DARK
MÖRKERSEENDE
(1970)

The Name

I grow sleepy during the car journey and I drive in under the trees at the side of the road. I curl up in the back seat and sleep. For how long? Hours. Darkness had come on.

Suddenly I'm awake and don't know where I am. Wide-awake, but it doesn't help. Where am I? WHO am I? I am something that wakens in a back seat, twists about in panic like a cat in a sack. Who?

At last my life returns. My name comes like an angel. Outside the walls a trumpet signal blows (as in the Leonora overture) and the rescuing footsteps come smartly down the overlong stairway. It is I! It is I!

But impossible to forget the fifteen second struggle in the hell of oblivion, a few metres from the main road, where the traffic glides past with its lights on.

A Few Minutes

The squat pine in the swamp holds up its crown: a dark rag.
But what you see is nothing
compared to the roots, the widespread, secretly creeping, immortal or
        half-mortal
root system.

I you she he also branch out.
Outside what one wills.
Outside the Metropolis.

A shower falls out of the milk-white summer sky.
It feels as if my five senses were linked to another creature
which moves stubbornly
as the brightly-clad runners in a stadium where the darkness streams
        down.

Breathing Space July

The man lying on his back under the high trees
is up there too. He rills out in thousands of twigs,
sways to and fro,
sits in an ejector seat that releases in slow motion.

The man down by the jetties narrows his eyes at the water.
The jetties grow old more quickly than people.
They have silver grey timber and stones in their stomachs.
The blinding light beats right in.

The man travelling all day in an open boat
over the glittering straits
will sleep at last inside a blue lamp
while the islands creep like large moths across the glass.

By the River

Talking with contemporaries I saw heard behind their faces
the stream
that flowed and flowed and pulled with it the willing and the unwilling.

And the creature with stuck-together eyes that wants
to go right down the rapids with the current
throws itself forward without trembling
in a furious hunger for simplicity.

The water pulls more and more swiftly

as where the river narrows and goes over
in the rapids – the place where I paused
after a journey through dry woods

one June evening: the radio gives the latest
on the special meeting: Kosygin, Eban.
A few thoughts drill despairingly.
A few people down in the village.

And under the suspension bridge the masses of water hurl
past. Here comes the timber. Some logs
shoot right out like torpedoes. Others turn
cross-wise, twirl sluggishly and helplessly away

and some nose against the river banks,
push among stones and rubbish, wedge fast
and pile up there like clasped hands

motionless in the uproar . . .

         I saw heard from the bridge
in a cloud of mosquitoes,
together with some boys. Their bicycles
buried in the greenery – only the horns
stuck up.

Outskirts

Men in overalls the same colour as the earth come up out of a ditch.
It is an intermediate place, stale-mate, neither city nor country.
The high cranes on the horizon want to take the great leap but the
       clocks don't want to.
Cement pipes, scattered around, lick up the light with dry tongues.
Car-body repair shops in one-time barns.
The stones throw their shadows abruptly like objects on the surface
       of the moon.
And these places just multiply.
Like what they bought with Judas' money: 'the potter's field, to bury
       strangers in'.

Traffic

The long-distance lorry with its trailer crawls through the mist
and is a large shadow of the dragonfly larva
which stirs in the mud of the lake-bed.

Headlights meet in a dripping forest.
One can't see the other's face.
The flood of light pours through the needles.

We come shadows vehicles from all directions
in the twilight, drive together behind each other
past each other, glide forward in a muffled clamour

out onto the plain where factories brood
and the buildings sink two millimetres
each year – the ground is eating them slowly.

Unidentified paws set their marks
on the brightest products dreamt up here.
The seeds try to live in the asphalt.

But first the chestnut trees, gloomy as if
they prepared a blossoming of iron gloves
instead of white clusters, and behind them

the company office – a faulty strip-light
blinks blinks. There's a secret door here. Unlock it –
look into the inverted periscope

downwards, to the openings, to the deep tubes
where the algae grow like the beards of the dead
and the Cleaner drifts in his dress of slime

with feebler and feebler strokes, on the point of suffocating.
And no one knows what will happen, only that the chain
perpetually breaks, perpetually joins together again.

Night Duty

1

Tonight I am down among the ballast.
I am one of the silent weights
which prevent the ship overturning!
Obscure faces in the darkness like stones.
They can only hiss: 'don't touch me'.

2

Other voices throng, the listener
glides like a lean shadow over the radio's
luminous band of stations.
The language marches in step with the executioners.
Therefore we must get a new language.

3

The wolf is here, friend for every hour
touching the windows with his tongue.
The valley is full of crawling axe-handles.
The night-flyer's din pours over the sky
sluggishly, like a wheel-chair with iron rims.

4

They are digging up the town. But it is silent now.
Under the elms in the churchyard:
an empty excavator. The scoop against the earth –
the gesture of a man who has fallen asleep at table
with his fist in front of him. – Bell-ringing.

The Open Window

I stood shaving one morning
before the open window
one storey up.
I switched the shaver on.
It began to purr.
It buzzed louder and louder.
It grew to an uproar.
It grew to a helicopter
and a voice – the pilot's – penetrated
through the din, shrieked:
'Keep your eyes open!
You're seeing all this for the last time.'
We rose.
Flew low over the summer.
So many things I liked, have they any weight?
Dozens of dialects of green.
And especially the red in the wooden house walls.
The beetles glistened in the dung, in the sun.
Cellars which were pulled up by the roots
came through the air.
Activity.
The printing-presses crawled.
Just now the people were
the only things that were still.
They observed a minute's silence.
And especially the dead in the country churchyard
were still
as if sitting for a picture in the infancy of the camera.
Fly low!
I didn't know where I
turned my head –
with a double field of vision
like a horse.

Preludes

1

I shy at something which comes shuffling cross-wise in the sleet.
Fragment of what will happen.
A wall broken loose. Something without eyes. Hard.
A face of teeth!
A solitary wall. Or is the house there
although I don't see it?
The future: an army of empty houses
picking its way forward in the sleet.

2

Two truths draw nearer each other. One comes from inside, one comes
        from outside
and where they meet we have a chance to see ourselves.

He who notices what is happening cries despairingly: 'Stop!
whatever you like, if only I avoid knowing myself.'

And there is a boat which wants to put in – it tries just here –
thousands of times it comes and tries.

Out of the forest gloom comes a long boat-hook, it is pushed in through
        the open window,
in among the party guests who danced themselves warm.

3

The flat where I lived the greater part of my life is to be cleared out.
It is now quite empty. The anchor has let go – although we are still
mourning it is the lightest flat in the whole city. The truth needs no
furniture. I have made a journey round life and come back to the starting-
point: a blown-out room. Things I have taken part in here show on the
walls like Egyptian paintings, scenes on the inside of a burial chamber.
But they are steadily being erased. For the light is too strong. The
windows have become bigger. The empty flat is a large telescope aimed
at the sky. It is silent as a quaker service. What can be heard are the
back-yard pigeons, their cooing.

Upright

In a moment of concentration I succeeded in catching the hen, I stood with it in my hands. Curiously, it did not feel properly alive: stiff, dry, an old white feather-trimmed woman's hat, which cried out truths from 1912. Thunder hung in the air. From the wooden planks a scent rose as when you open a photo album so aged that you can no longer identify the portraits.

I carried the hen into the enclosure and let her go. Suddenly she was very much alive, knew where she was and ran according to the rules. The hen-yard is full of taboos. But the earth around is full of love and tenacity. A low stone wall half overgrown with greenery. When dusk comes the stones begin to gleam faintly with the hundred-year-old warmth from the hands that built.

The winter has been hard but now summer is here and the earth wants to have us upright. Free but wary, as when you stand up in a slim boat. A memory from Africa occurs to me: on the shore at Chari, many boats, a very friendly atmosphere, the almost blue-black people with three parallel scars on each cheek (the SARA tribe). I am welcomed aboard – a canoe of dark wood. It is surprisingly rickety, also when I squat down. A balancing act. If the heart lies on the left side you must incline your head a little to the right, nothing in the pockets, no large gestures, all rhetoric must be left behind. Just this: rhetoric is impossible here. The canoe glides out on the water.

The Bookcase

It was fetched from the dead woman's apartment. It stood empty for a few days, empty, until I filled it with books, all the bound ones, the heavy ones. In doing so, I had let in the nether world. Something came from underneath, rose slowly and inexorably like a massive column of mercury. One was not allowed to turn one's head away.

The dark volumes, closed faces. They are like Algerians who stood at the Friedrichstrasse checkpoint and waited for the Volkspolizei to examine their passports. My own passport has long since lain among the glass cages. And the haze which was in Berlin in those days is also inside the bookcase. In there lies an old despair that tastes of Passchendaele and the Versailles Peace, that tastes even older. The dark heavy tomes – I come back to them – they are in reality a kind of passport and they are so thick because they have collected so many stamps through the centuries. Evidently you cannot travel with enough heavy baggage, now when you set off, when you at last . . .

All the old historians are there, they rise up there and look into our family. Nothing is heard but the lips are moving all the time behind the glass ('Passchendaele' . . .). It makes you think of an aged civil service department (a pure ghost-story follows), a building where portraits of long since dead men hang behind glass and one morning there was vapour on the inside of the glass. They had begun to breathe during the night.

The bookcase is still more powerful. The glances straight across the border! A gleaming membrane, the gleaming membrane on a dark river which the room must see itself in. And one is not allowed to turn one's head away.

PATHS
STIGAR
(1973)

To Friends behind a Frontier

1

I wrote so meagrely to you. But what I couldn't write
swelled and swelled like an old-fashioned airship
and drifted away at last through the night sky.

2

The letter is now at the censor's. He lights his lamp.
In the glare my words fly up like monkeys on a grille,
rattle it, stop, and bare their teeth.

3

Read between the lines. We'll meet in 200 years
when the microphones in the hotel walls are forgotten
and can at last sleep, become trilobites.

From the Thaw of 1966

Headlong headlong waters; roaring; old hypnosis.
The river swamps the car-cemetery, glitters
behind the masks.
I hold tight to the bridge railing.
The bridge: a big iron bird sailing past death.

Sketch in October

The tug is freckled with rust. What's it doing here so far inland?
It's a heavy extinguished lamp in the cold.
But the trees have wild colours: signals to the other shore.
As if someone wanted to be fetched.

On my way home I see mushrooms sprouting through the grass.
They are the fingers, stretching for help, of someone
who has for long sobbed alone in the darkness down there.
We are the earth's.

Further In

On the main road into the city
when the sun is low.
The traffic thickens, crawls.
It is a sluggish dragon glittering.
I am one of the dragon's scales.
Suddenly the red sun is
right in the middle of the windscreen
streaming in.
I am transparent
and writing becomes visible
inside me
words in invisible ink
which appear
when the paper is held to the fire!
I know I must get far away
straight through the city and then
further until it is time to go out
and walk far in the forest.
Walk in the footprints of the badger.
It gets dark, difficult to see.
In there on the moss lie stones.
One of the stones is precious.
It can change everything
it can make the darkness shine.
It is a switch for the whole country.
Everything depends on it.
Look at it, touch it . . .

The Outpost

I'm ordered out in a heap of stones
like a distinguished corpse from the iron age.
The others are back in the tent sleeping
stretched out like spokes in a wheel.

In the tent the stove rules: a big snake
that has swallowed a ball of fire and hisses.
But out in the spring night it is silent
among cold stones that are waiting for day.

Out there in the cold I begin to fly
like a shaman, I fly to her body
with its white marks from her bikini –
we were out in the sun. The moss was warm.

I flit over warm moments
but can't stop for long.
They're whistling me back through space –
I crawl out from the stones. Here and now.

Mission: to be where I am.
Even in that ridiculous, deadly serious
role – I am the place
where creation is working itself out.

Daybreak, the sparse tree-trunks
are coloured now, the frost-bitten
spring flowers form a silent search party
for someone who has vanished in the dark.

But to be where I am. And to wait.
I am anxious, stubborn, confused.
Coming events, they're there already!
I know it. They're outside:

a murmuring crowd outside the gate.
They can pass only one by one.
They want in. Why? They're coming
one by one. I am the turnstile.

Along the Radius

I

The ice-bound river is blazing with sun
here is the world's roof
silence.

I'm sitting on an upturned boat on the bank
swallowing the drug of silence
spinning gently.

II

A wheel spreads out endlessly, turns.
Here is the centre, almost
still.

Further out, perceptible movement: the steps in the snow
the writing which shuffles along
the façades.

The rumbling traffic on the highways
and the silent traffic
of ghosts.

And further out: the tragic masks in the head-wind
in the whine of speed – further out:
the rush

where the last words of love evaporate –
the drips that creep
on the steel wings –

profiles that cry out – the suspended head-phones
chatter at each other –
kamikaze!

III

The ice-bound river glitters and is silent.
The shadows lie deep here
and voiceless.

My steps here were explosions in the ground
which the silence paints over
paints over.

Looking through the Ground

The white sun is soaking through the smog.
The light drips, gropes its way down

to my deep-down eyes that are resting
deep under the city looking up

seeing the city from below: streets, foundations –
like aerial photos of a city in war

the wrong way round – a mole photo:
silent squares in sombre colours.

The decisions are taken there. No telling
bones of the dead from bones of the living.

The sunlight's volume is turned up,
it floods into flight-cabins and peapods.

December Evening 1972

Here I come, the invisible man, perhaps employed
by a Great Memory to live right now. And I am driving past

the locked-up white church – a wooden saint is standing in there
smiling, helpless, as if they had taken away his glasses.

He is alone. Everything else is now, now, now. The law of gravity
          pressing us
against our work by day and against our beds by night. The war.

The Dispersed Congregation

I

We made an effort, showing our homes.
The visitor thought: you live well.
The slum is within you.

II

Inside the church: vaults and columns
white as plaster, like the plaster bandage
round the broken arm of faith.

III

Inside the church: the begging bowl
that raises itself from the floor
and goes along the pews.

IV

But the church bells must go under the earth.
They hang in the sewage tunnels.
They toll under our steps.

V

The sleepwalker Nicodemus on his way
to the Address. Who has the address?
Don't know. But that's where we're going.

Late May

Apple trees and cherry trees in bloom help the town to soar
in the sweet dirty May night, white life-jacket, my thoughts range out.
Grasses and weeds with silent stubborn wing-beats.
The letter-box shines calmly, what's written can't be taken back.

Soft cool wind gets through my shirt and gropes for my heart.
Apple trees and cherry trees, they laugh silently at Solomon
they blossom in my tunnel. I need them
not to forget but to remember.

Elegy

I open the first door.
It's a large sunlit room.
A heavy car goes past in the street
and makes the porcelain tremble.

I open door number two.
Friends! You drank the darkness
and became visible.

Door number three. A narrow hotel-room.
Outlook on a back street.
A lamp sparking on the asphalt.
Beautiful slag of experiences.

BALTICS

ÖSTERSJÖAR

(1974)

I

It was before the age of the radio masts.

Grandfather was a new-made pilot. In the almanac he wrote down the
        vessels he piloted –
names, destinations, draught.
Examples from 1884:
Steamer Tiger Capt. Rowan 16 ft Hull Gefle Furusund
Brigg Ocean Capt. Andersen 8 ft Sandöfjord Hernösand Furusund
Steamer St Pettersburg Capt Libenberg 11 ft Stettin Libau Sandhamn

He took them out to the Baltic, through the marvellous labyrinth of
        islands and waters.
And those who met on board and were carried by the same hull for
        a few hours, or days,
how much did they come to know each other?
Conversations in misspelt English, understanding and misunderstanding
        but very little conscious falsehood.
How much did they come to know each other?

When it was thick fog: half-speed, half blind ahead. At one single stride
        the cape came out of the invisible and was right on them.
Every other minute a bellowing signal. His eyes read straight into the
        invisible.
(Had he the labyrinth in his head?)
The minutes passed.
Shallows and skerries he memorised like psalm verses.
And that feeling of we're-just-here which must be kept, like carrying
        a brimful pail without spilling a drop.

A glance down in the engine-room.
The compound machine long-lived as a human heart toiled with great
        supple bouncing movements, acrobats of steel, and the smells
        came up like out of a kitchen.

II

The wind is in the pine forest. Sighing heavily and lightly.
The Baltic is sighing in the middle of the island also, far within the
      forest you are out on the open sea.
The old woman hated the sighing in the trees. Her face stiffened in
      melancholy when the wind blew up:
'We must think about the men out in the boats.'
But she heard something else as well in the sighing, as I do, we are kin.
(We are walking together. She's been dead for thirty years.)
There's sighing, yes and no, understanding and misunderstanding.
There's sighing, three sound children, one in a sanatorium and two dead.
The great current that blows life into some flames and blows others
      out. The conditions.
Sighing: Save me, O God; for the waters are come in unto my soul.
You go on, listening, and then reach a point where the frontiers open
or rather
where everything becomes a frontier. An open place sunk in darkness.
      The people stream out from the faintly lit buildings round about.
      Murmuring.

A new breath of wind and the place lies desolate and silent again.

A new breath of wind, sighing about other shores.
It's about war.
It's about places where citizens are under control,
where their thoughts are made with emergency exits,
where a conversation between friends really becomes a test of what
      friendship means.
And when you are with people you don't know so well. Control.
      A certain sincerity is in place
if only you don't take your eyes off what's drifting on the outskirts
      of the conversation: something dark, a dark stain.
Something that can drift in
and destroy everything. Don't take your eyes off it!
What can we compare it to? A mine?
No, that would be too concrete. And almost too peaceful – for on our
      coast most of the stories about mines have a happy ending, the
      terror short-lived.
As in this story from the light-ship: 'In the autumn of 1915 we slept
      uneasily . . .' etc. A drift-mine was sighted

as it drifted slowly towards the light-ship, then sank and resurfaced,
      sometimes hidden by the waters, sometimes glimpsed like a
      spy in a crowd.
The crew were in a sweat and shot at it with rifles. No use. At last they
      put out a boat and made fast a long line to it and carefully and
      slowly towed it to the experts.
Afterwards they set up the dark shell of the mine in a sandy plantation
      as an ornament
together with the shells of Strombus Gigas from the West Indies.

And the sea wind is in the dry pines further away, hurrying over the
      churchyard sand,
past the leaning stones, the pilots' names.
The dry sighing
of great doors opening and great doors closing.

III

In the half-dark corner of a Gotland church, in a glimmer of soft mildew
there's a sandstone font – 12th century – the mason's name
is still there, shining out
like a row of teeth in a mass grave:
                HEGWALDR
                        the name's left. And his pictures
here and on the sides of other pots, human swarms, figures stepping out
      of the stone.
There the eyes' kernels of good and evil are split.
Herod at table: the roasted cock flies up and crows 'Christus natus est'
      – the waiter was executed –
close by, the child is born, under clusters of faces dignified and helpless
      as those of young apes.
And the fleeing steps of the pious
echoing over dragon-scaled sewer openings.
(The images stronger in memory than when seen direct, strongest
when in memory the font turns like a slow rumbling merry-go-round).
Nowhere lee. Everywhere risk.
As it was. As it is.
Only in there is there peace, in the vessel's water that no one sees,

but on the outer walls the battle is raging.
And peace can come drop by drop, perhaps at night
when we know nothing
or when you are lying in a hospital ward on a drip.

People, beasts, ornaments.
There is no landscape. Ornaments.

Mr B, my amiable travelling companion, in exile,
released from Robben Island, says:
'I envy you. I feel nothing for nature.
But *figures in a landscape*, that says something to me.'

Here are figures in a landscape.
A photo from 1865. The steamer is at the pier in the sound.
Five figures. A lady in a bright crinoline, like a bell, like a flower.
The men are like extras in a rustic play.
They're all beautiful, irresolute, in the process of being rubbed out.
They step ashore for a little while. They're being rubbed out.
The steam launch is an extinct model –
high funnel, sunroof, narrow hull –
it's utterly foreign, a UFO that's landed.
Everything else in the photo is shockingly real:
the ripples on the water,
the opposite shore –
I can stroke my hand over the rough rock-faces,
I can hear the sighing in the spruces.
It's near. It's
today.
The waves are topical.

Now a hundred years later. The waves are coming in from no-man's
             water
and break on the stones.
I walk along the shore. Walking along the shore is not as it was.
You have to take in too much, keep up many conversations at once,
             you have thin walls.
Each thing has acquired a new shadow behind the usual shadow
and you hear it trailing along even in total darkness.

It's night.

The strategic planetarium rotates. The lenses stare in the dark.
The night sky is full of numbers and they are fed
into a twinkling cupboard
a piece of furniture
where there lives the energy of a locust swarm that denudes the acreage
     of Somaliland in half an hour.

I don't know if we are at the beginning or coming to the end.
The summing-up can't be done, the summing-up is impossible.
The summing-up is the mandrake –
(See the encyclopedia of superstitions:
                MANDRAKE
                             miracle-working plant
which when torn out of the ground gave off such an appalling scream
a man would drop dead. A dog had to do it.)

IV

From leeward,
close-ups.

Bladderwrack: The weed-forests shine in the clear water, they are
     young, you want to emigrate there, lie down full-length on your
     mirror image and sink to a certain depth – the weed that holds
     itself up with air-bladders as we hold ourselves up with ideas.

Bullhead: The fish who is a toad who wanted to become a butterfly and
     succeeded a third of the way, hides himself in the seaweed but
     is drawn up in the nets, hooked fast by his pathetic spikes and
     warts – when you disentangle it from the meshes your hands
     are gleaming with slime.

Rockface. Out on the sun-warmed lichens the insects scurry, they're
     in a rush like second-hands – the pine throws a shadow, it
     moves slowly like an hour-hand – inside me time stands still,
     an infinity of time, the time required to forget all languages
     and to invent perpetuum mobile.

On the lee-side you can hear the grass growing: a faint drumming from
     underneath, a faint roar of millions of little gas-flames, that's
     what it's like to hear the grass growing.

And now: the width of water, without doors, the open frontier
that grows broader and broader
the further you reach out.

There are days when the Baltic is a calm endless roof.
Dream your naive dreams then about someone coming crawling on the
          roof trying to sort out the flag-lines,
trying to hoist
the rag –

the flag which is so eroded by the wind and blackened by the funnels
          and bleached by the sun it can be everyone's.

But it's a long way to Liepaja.

V

July 30th. The strait has become eccentric – swarming with jellyfish
          today for the first time in years, they pump themselves forward
          calmly and patiently, they belong to the same line: *Aurelia*, they
          drift like flowers after a sea-burial, if you take them out of the
          water all their form vanishes, as when an indescribable truth
          is lifted out of silence and formulated to an inert mass, but they
          are untranslatable, they must stay in their own element.

August 2nd. Something wants to be said but the words don't agree.
Something which can't be said,
aphasia,
there are no words but perhaps a style . . .

You can wake up in the small hours
jot down a few words
on the nearest paper, a newsprint margin
(the words radiate meaning!)
but in the morning: the same words now say nothing, scrawls,
          slips-of-the-tongue.
Or fragments of the high nocturnal style that drew past?

Music comes to a man, he's a composer, he's played, makes a career,
       becomes Conservatory Director.
The climate changes, he's condemned by the authorities.
His pupil K. is set up as prosecutor.
He's threatened, degraded, removed.
After a few years the disgrace lessens, he's rehabilitated.
Then, cerebral haemorrhage: paralysis on the right side with aphasia,
       can grasp only short phrases, says the wrong words.
Beyond the reach of eulogy or execration.
But the music's left, he goes on composing in his own style,
for the rest of his days he becomes a medical sensation.

He wrote music to texts he no longer understood –
in the same way
we express something through our lives
in the humming chorus full of mistaken words.

The death-lectures went on for several terms. I attended
together with people I didn't know
(who are you?)
- then each went his own way, profiles.

I looked at the sky and at the earth and straight ahead
and since then I've been writing a long letter to the dead
on a typewriter with no ribbon just a horizon line
so the words knock in vain and nothing sticks.

I pause with my hand on the door-handle, take the pulse of the house.
The walls are so full of life
(the children don't dare to sleep alone in the little room upstairs –
       what makes me safe makes them uneasy).

August 3rd. Out there in the damp grass
a greeting shuffles from the Middle Ages, the Edible Snail,
subtle gleaming grey-and-yellow, with his house aslant,
introduced by monks who liked their *escargots* – the Franciscans were
       here,
broke stone and burned lime, the island became theirs in 1288, a gift
       of King Magnus
('Almes fordoth all wykkednes / And quenchyth synne and makyth
       hyt les')
the forest fell, the ovens burned, the lime was shipped in for the
       building of the monastery...

     Sister snail
almost motionless in the grass, the antennae are sucked in
and rolled out, disturbances and hesitation...
How like myself in my searching!

The wind that's been blowing carefully all day
– the blades of grass on the outer skerries are all counted –
has lain down peacefully at the heart of the island. The match-flame
    stands straight.
The sea-painting and the forest-painting darken together.
The foliage on the five-storey trees turns black.
'Each summer is the last.' Empty words
for the creatures in the late summer midnight
where the crickets whirr their sewing-machines frantically
and the Baltic is close
and the lonely water-tap rises among the wild roses
like the statue of a horseman. The water tastes of iron.

VI

Grandmother's story before it's forgotten: her parents die young
father first. When the widow knows the disease will take her too
she walks from house to house, sails from island to island
with her daughter. 'Who can take Maria?' A strange house
on the other side of the bay takes her. There they have the means.
But that didn't make them good. The mask of piety cracks.
Maria's childhood ends too early, she's an unpaid servant
in perpetual coldness. Year after year. Perpetual seasickness
during the long stints of rowing, solemn terror
at table, the looks, the pike-skin scrunching
in her mouth: be grateful, be grateful.
         She never looked back
but because of that she could see what was new
and catch hold of it.
Out of encirclement.

I remember her. I would press close to her
and at the moment of death (the moment of crossing?) she sent out a
    thought
so that I – a five year old – understood what happened
half an hour before they rang.

Her I remember. But on the next brown photo
the unknown man –
dated by his clothes to the middle of last century.
A man around thirty: the vigorous eyebrows,
the face looking straight into my eyes
and whispering: 'here I am'.
But who 'I' am
there's no one any more who remembers. No one.

TB? Isolation?

Once coming up from the sea
on the stony slope steaming with grass he stopped
and felt the black bandage on his eyes.

Here, behind dense thickets – is it the island's oldest house?
The low, two-centuries-old fisherman's hut, log-cabin style, with
          heavy coarse grey timbers.
And the modern brass padlock has clicked it all together and shines
          like the ring in the nose of an old bull
who refuses to get up.
So much wood crouching. On the roof the ancient tiles which have
          slipped downways and crossways over each other
(the original pattern deranged over the years by the rotation of the
          earth)
it reminds me of something . . . I was there . . . wait: it's the old Jewish
          cemetery in Prague
where the dead live more packed than they were in life, the stones
          packed packed.
So much love encircled! The tiles with their lichen-script in an unknown
          tongue
are the stones in the ghetto cemetery of the archipelago folk, the stones
          raised and tumbled. –
The hovel is lit up
with all those who were driven by a certain wave, by a certain wind
right out here to their fates.

THE TRUTH-BARRIER
SANNINGSBARRIÄREN
(1978)

Citoyens

The night after the accident I dreamt of a pock-marked man
who walked through the alleys singing.
Danton!
Not the other one – Robespierre doesn't take such walks,
Robespierre spends a careful hour each morning on his toilette,
the rest of the day he devotes to The People.
In the paradise of the pamphlets, among the machines of virtue.
Danton –
or the man who wore his mask –
seemed to be standing on stilts.
I saw his face from beneath.
Like the scarred moon,
half in light, half in mourning.
I wanted to say something.
A weight in the breast, the plummet
that makes the clocks go,
the hands turn: year 1, year 2 . . .
A sharp scent like sawdust in the tiger-stalls.
And – as always in dreams – no sun.
But the walls were shining
in the alleys that curved
down to the waiting-room, the curved room,
the waiting-room where we all . . .

The Crossing-Place

Ice-wind in my eyes and the suns dance
in the kaleidoscope of tears as I cross
the street that's followed me so long, the street
where Greenland-summer shines from puddles.

Around me the whole strength of the street swarms,
power that remembers nothing, wants nothing.
For a thousand years, in the earth deep
under traffic the unborn forest quietly waits.

I get the idea that the street can see me.
Its sight is so dim the sun itself
is a grey ball in a black space.
But right now I am shining! The street sees me.

The Clearing

Deep in the forest there's an unexpected clearing which can be reached
only by someone who has lost his way.

The clearing is enclosed in a forest that is choking itself. Black trunks
with the ashy beard-stubble of lichen. The trees are screwed tightly
together and are dead right up to the tops, where a few solitary green
twigs touch the light. Beneath them: shadow brooding on shadow, and
the swamp growing.

But in the open space the grass is strangely green and living. There
are big stones lying here as if they'd been arranged. They must be the
foundation stones of a house, but I could be wrong. Who lived here?
No one can tell us. The names exist somewhere in an archive that no
one opens (it's only archives that stay young). The oral tradition has
died and with it the memories. The gypsy people remember but those
who have learnt to write forget. Write down, and forget.

The homestead murmurs with voices, it is the centre of the world.
But the inhabitants die or move out, the chronicle breaks off. Desolate
for many years. And the homestead becomes a sphinx. At last every-
thing's gone, except the foundation stones.

Somehow I've been here before, but now I must go. I dive in among
the thickets. I can push my way through only with one step forward and
two to the side, like a chess knight. Bit by bit the forest thins and
lightens. My steps get longer. A footpath creeps towards me. I am back
in the communications network.

On the humming electricity-post a beetle is sitting in the sun. Beneath
the shining wing-covers its wings are folded up as ingeniously as a
parachute packed by an expert.

How the Late Autumn Night Novel Begins

The ferry-boat smells of oil and something rattles all the time like an obsession. The spotlight's turned on. We're pulling in to the jetty. I'm the only one who wants off here. 'Need the gangway?' No. I take a long tottering stride right into the night and stand on the jetty, on the island. I feel wet and unwieldy, a butterfly just crept out of its cocoon, the plastic bags in each hand hang like misshapen wings. I turn round and see the boat gliding away with its shining windows, then grope my way towards the house which has been empty for so long. There's no one in any of the houses round about . . . It's good to fall asleep here. I lie on my back and don't know if I'm asleep or awake. Some books I've read pass by like old sailing ships on their way to the Bermuda triangle to vanish without trace . . . I hear a hollow sound, an absent-minded drumming. An object the wind keeps knocking against something the earth holds still. If the night is not just an absence of light, if the night really *is* something, then it's that sound. Stethoscope noises from a slow heart, it beats, goes silent for a time, comes back. As if the creature were moving in a zigzag across the Frontier. Or someone knocking in a wall, someone who belongs to the other world but was left behind here, knocking, wanting back. Too late. Couldn't get down there, couldn't get up there, couldn't get aboard . . . The other world is this world too. Next morning I see a sizzling golden-brown branch. A crawling stack of roots. Stones with faces. The forest is full of abandoned monsters which I love.

To Mats and Laila

The Dateline stays still between Samoa and Tonga but the Midnight-line glides forward over the ocean and the islands and the roofs of cabins. They're sleeping there, on the other side. Here in Värmland it's broad daylight, a day in early summer with a burning sun – I've thrown aside my luggage. A swim in the sky, the air's so blue . . . Then suddenly I see the ridges on the other side of the lake: they are clean-cut. Like the shaved parts of a patient's crown before he has a brain operation. It's been there all the time, I haven't seen it until now. Blinkers and a stiff neck . . . The journey continues. The landscape is now full of hatching and lines, like the old engravings where people moved about small between hills and mountains which resembled anthills and villages which were also thousands of strokes. And each man-ant brought his own little stroke to add to the big engraving, there was no proper centre but everything was alive. Something else: the figures are small but each has his own face, the engraver has not denied them that – they are no ants. Most of them are simple people but they can write their names. Proteus on the other hand is a modern man who expresses himself fluently in every style, comes with a "straight message" or empty flourishes depending on which gang he belongs to at that moment. He can't write his name. He shies away from it like the werewolf from the silver bullet. They don't ask for it either, the hydra of the Company or the hydra of the State . . . The journey continues. In this house there lives a man who became desperate one evening and shot at the empty hammock swaying above the grass. And the Midnight-line comes closer, it'll soon have covered half its course. (And don't make out I want to turn the clock back.) Tiredness will stream in through the hole left by the sun . . . For me it's never happened that the diamond of a certain moment cut an indelible score across the world-picture. No, it was wear and tear that rubbed out the bright strange smile. But something's in the process of becoming visible again, it's being worn *in*, begins to look like a smile, no one knows what it's worth. Unaccounted for. There's someone catches at my arm each time I try to write.

From the Winter of 1947

Days at school, that muffled thronging fortress.
At dusk I walked home under the shop-signs.
Then the whispering without lips: 'Wake up, sleepwalker!'
And every object pointed to The Room.

Fifth floor, a view of the yard. The lamp burned
in a circle of terror night after night.
I sat in bed without eyelids, saw filmstrips
filmstrips with the thoughts of insane people.

As if it were necessary . . .
As if the last childhood were being broken up
to make it pass through the grid.
As if it were necessary . . .

I read in books of glass but saw only the other:
the stains pushing through the wallpaper.
It was the living dead
who wanted their portraits painted . . .

Till dawn when the dustmen came
clattering the metal bins down there.
The back yard's peaceful grey bells
ringing me to sleep.

Schubertiana

1

In the evening darkness in a place outside New York, an outlook point
        where one single glance will encompass the homes of eight
        million people.
The giant city over there is a long shimmering drift, a spiral galaxy
        seen from the side.
Within the galaxy coffee-cups are pushed across the counter, the
        shop-windows beg from passers-by, a flurry of shoes that leave
        no prints.
The climbing fire escapes, the lift doors that glide shut, behind doors
        with police locks a perpetual seethe of voices.
Slouched bodies doze in subway coaches, the hurtling catacombs.
I know too – without statistics – that right now Schubert is being played
        in some room over there and that for someone the notes are
        more real than all the rest.

2

The endless expanses of the human brain are crumpled to the size
        of a fist.
In April the swallow returns to last year's nest under the guttering of
        this very barn in this very parish.
She flies from Transvaal, passes the equator, flies for six weeks over
        two continents, makes for precisely this vanishing dot in the
        land-mass.
And the man who catches the signals from a whole life in a few ordinary
        chords for five strings,

who makes a river flow through the eye of a needle,
is a stout young gentleman from Vienna known to his friends as 'The
          Mushroom', who slept with his glasses on
and stood at his writing desk punctually of a morning.
And then the wonderful centipedes of his manuscript were set in
motion.

3

The string quintet is playing. I walk home through warm forests with
          the ground springy under me,
curl up like an embryo, fall asleep, roll weightless into the future,
          suddenly feel that the plants have thoughts.

4

So much we have to trust, simply to live through our daily day without
          sinking through the earth!
Trust the piled snow clinging to the mountain slope above the village.
Trust the promises of silence and the smile of understanding, trust
          that the accident telegram isn't for us and that the sudden
          axe-blow from within won't come.
Trust the axles that carry us on the highway in the middle of the three
          hundred times life-size bee-swarm of steel.
But none of that is really worth our confidence.
The five strings say we can trust something else. And they keep us
          company part of the way there.
As when the time-switch clicks off in the stairwell and the fingers –
          trustingly – follow the blind handrail that finds its way in the
          darkness.

5

We squeeze together at the piano and play with four hands in F minor,
          two coachmen on the same coach, it looks a little ridiculous.
The hands seem to be moving resonant weights to and fro, as if we
          were tampering with the counterweights
in an effort to disturb the great scale arm's terrible balance: joy and
          suffering weighing exactly the same.
Annie said, 'This music is so heroic,' and she's right.
But those whose eyes enviously follow men of action, who secretly
          despise themselves for not being murderers,
don't recognise themselves here,

and the many who buy and sell people and believe that everyone can
        be bought, don't recognise themselves here.
Not their music. The long melody that remains itself in all its
        transformations, sometimes glittering and pliant, sometimes
        rugged and strong, snail-track and steel wire.
The perpetual humming that follows us – now –
up
the depths.

The Gallery

I stayed overnight at a motel by the E3.
In my room a smell I'd felt before
in the oriental halls of a museum:

masks Tibetan Japanese on a pale wall.

But it's not masks now, it's faces

forcing through the white wall of oblivion
to breathe, to ask about something.
I lie awake watching them struggle
and disappear and return.

Some lend each other features, exchange faces
far inside me
where oblivion and memory wheel-and-deal.

They force through oblivion's second coat
the white wall
they fade-out fade-in.

Here is a sorrow that doesn't call itself sorrow.

Welcome to the authentic galleries!
Welcome to the authentic galleys!
The authentic grilles!

The karate boy who paralysed someone
is still dreaming of fast money.

This woman keeps buying things
to toss in the hungry mouth of the vacuum
sneaking up behind her.

Mr X doesn't dare go out.
A dark stockade of ambiguous people
stands between him
and the steadily retreating horizon.

She who once fled from Karelia
she who could laugh . . .
now shows herself
but dumb, petrified, a statue from Sumer.

As when I was ten and came home late.
In the stairwell the light switched off
but the lift I stood in was bright, it rose
like a diving-bell through black depths
floor by floor while imagined faces
pressed against the grille . . .

But the faces are not imagined now, they are real.

I lie straight out like a cross-street.

Many step out from the white mist.
We touched each other once – we did!

A long bright carbolic-scented corridor.
The wheelchair. The teenage girl
learning to talk after the car-crash.

He who tried to call out under water
and the world's cold mass poured in
through nose and mouth.

Voices in the microphone said: Speed is power
speed is power!
Play the game, the show must go on!

We move through our career stiffly, step by step,
it's like a Noh play
with masks, high-pitched song: It's me, it's me!
The one who's failed
is represented by a rolled-up blanket.

An artist said: Before, I was a planet
with its own dense atmosphere.
Entering rays were broken into rainbows.
Perpetual raging thunderstorms, within.

Now I'm extinct and dry and open.
I no longer have childlike energy.
I have a hot side and a cold side.

No rainbows.

I stayed overnight in the echoing house.
Many want to come in through the walls
but most of them can't make it:

they're overcome by the white hiss of oblivion.

Anonymous singing drowns in the walls.
Discreet tappings that don't want to be heard
drawn-out sighs
my old repartees creeping homelessly.

Listen to society's mechanical self-reproaches
the voice of the big fan
like the artificial wind in mine tunnels
six hundred metres down.

Our eyes keep wide open under the bandages.

If I could at least make them realise
that this trembling beneath us
means we are on a bridge.

Often I have to stand motionless.
I am the knife-thrower's partner at a circus!
Questions I tossed aside in rage
come whining back

don't hit me, but nail down my shape
my rough outline
and stay in place when I've walked away.

Often I have to be silent. Voluntarily!
Because 'the last word' is said again and again.
Because good-day and good-bye . . .
Because this very day . . .

Because the margins rise at last
over their brims
and flood the text.

I stayed overnight at the sleepwalker's motel.
Many faces here are desperate
others smoothed out
after the pilgrim's walk through oblivion.

They breathe vanish struggle back again
they look past me
they all want to reach the icon of justice.

It happens rarely
that one of us really *sees* the other:

a person shows himself for an instant
as in a photograph but clearer
and in the background
something which is bigger than his shadow.

He's standing full-length before a mountain.
It's more a snail's shell than a mountain.
It's more a house than a snail's shell.
It's not a house but has many rooms.
It's indistinct but overwhelming.
He grows out of it, it out of him.
It's his life, it's his labyrinth.

Below Zero

We are at a party that doesn't love us. At last the party lets its mask drop and shows itself for what it really is: a marshalling yard. Cold colossi stand on rails in the mist. A piece of chalk has scribbled on the wagon doors.

It shouldn't be said but there is much suppressed violence here. That's why the components are so heavy. And why it's so hard to see something else that's there too: a little reflection from a mirror, flitting on the house-walls and gliding through the unknowing forest of glimmering faces, a biblical text which was never written: 'Come unto me, for I am full of contradictions like you.'

Tomorrow I am working in another town. I swish towards it through the morning hour which is like a big dark-blue cylinder. Orion hangs above the ground-frost. Children are standing in a silent cluster waiting for the school bus, children no one prays for. The light is growing as slowly as our hair.

The Boat and the Village

A Portuguese fishing-boat, blue, the wash rolls up the Atlantic a little.
A blue speck far out, but still I'm there, the six aboard don't notice
    we're seven.

I saw such a boat being built, it lay like a big lute without strings
in Poor Valley, the village where they wash and wash in fury, patience,
    melancholy.

The shore black with people, some meeting breaking up, the
    loudspeakers being carried away.
Soldiers led the speaker's Mercedes through the crush, words
    drummed on its metal sides.

The Black Mountains

At the next bend the bus broke free of the mountain's cold shadow,
turned its nose to the sun and crept roaring upwards.
We were packed in. The dictator's bust was there too,
wrapped in newspaper. A bottle passed from mouth to mouth.
Death, the birthmark, was growing on all of us, quicker on some,
        slower on others.
Up in the mountains the blue sea caught up with the sky.

Homewards

A telephone call ran out in the night and glittered over the countryside
        and in the suburbs.
Afterwards I slept uneasily in the hotel bed.
I was like the needle in a compass carried through the forest by an
        orienteer with a thumping heart.

After a Long Drought

The summer's grey right now strange evening.
The rain steals down from the sky
and lands quietly as if
it had to overpower someone sleeping.

The water-rings jostle on the bay's surface
and that is the only surface there is –
the other is height and depth
soar and sink.

Two pine-stems
shoot up and end in long hollow signal-drums.
Gone are the cities and the sun.
The thunder's in the tall grass.

It's possible to ring up the mirage island.
It's possible to hear the grey voice.
Iron-ore is honey for the thunder.
It's possible to live with one's code.

A Place in the Forest

On the way there a pair of startled wings clattered up, that was all. You go there alone. There is a tall building which consists entirely of cracks, a building which is perpetually tottering but can never collapse. The thousand-fold sun floats in through the cracks. In this play of light an inverted law of gravity prevails: the house is anchored in the sky and whatever falls, falls upwards. You can turn round there. There you are allowed to grieve. You can dare to see certain old truths which are otherwise kept packed, in storage. The roles I have, deep down, float up there, hang like the dried skulls in the ancestral cabin on some out-of-the-way Melanesian islet. A childlike aura round the gruesome trophies. So mild it is, in the forest.

Funchal

The fish-restaurant on the beach, simple, a shack built by ship-wrecked people. Many turn away at the door, but not the gusts from the sea. A shadow stands in his reeking cabin frying two fish according to an old recipe from Atlantis, small explosions of garlic, oil running over the tomato slices. Every bite says that the ocean wishes us well, a humming from the deeps.

She and I look into each other. Like climbing up the wild blossoming hillsides without feeling the least tiredness. We're on the side of the animals, we're welcome, we don't get older. But over the years we've experienced so much together, we remember that, also times we were good for nothing (as when we queued up to give blood to the flourishing giant – he'd ordered transfusions), things that would've separated us if they hadn't brought us closer, and things we forgot together – but they have not forgotten us. They've become stones, dark ones and light ones. Stones in a scattered mosaic. And now it happens: the bits fly together, the mosaic is visible. It's waiting for us. It's shining from the wall in our hotel room, a design both violent and tender, perhaps a face, we haven't time to notice everything as we pull off our clothes . . .

At dusk we go out. The cape's enormous dark blue paw lies sprawled in the sea. We step into the human whirlpool, pushed around in a friendly way, soft controls, everyone chattering in that foreign language. 'No man is an island.' We become stronger through them, but also through ourselves. Through that within us which the other can't see. Which can meet only itself. The innermost paradox, the garage flower, the ventilator to the good darkness. A drink that bubbles in empty glasses. A loudspeaker that sends out silence. A pathway that grows over again behind each step. A book that can be read only in the dark.

THE WILD MARKET-PLACE

DET VILDA TORGET

(1983)

Brief Pause in the Organ Recital

The organ stops playing and it's deathly quiet in the church, but only
    for a couple of seconds.
And the faint rumbling penetrates from the traffic out there, that
    greater organ.

For we are surrounded by the murmuring of the traffic, it flows along
    the cathedral walls.
The outer world glides there like a transparent film and with shadows
    struggling pianissimo.

And as if it were part of the street noise I hear one of my pulses beating
    in the silence,
I hear my blood circulating, the cascade that hides inside me, that
    I walk about with,

and as close as my blood and as far away as a memory from when
    I was four
I hear the trailer that rumbles past and makes the six-hundred-year-old
    walls tremble.

This could hardly be less like a mother's lap, yet at the moment I am
    a child,
hearing the grown-ups talking far away, the voices of the winners and
    the losers mingling.

On the blue benches a sparse congregation. And the pillars rise like
    strange trees:
no roots (only the common floor) and no crown (only the common
    roof).

I relive a dream. That I'm standing alone in a churchyard. Everywhere
    heather glows
as far as the eye can reach. Who am I waiting for? A friend. Why doesn't
    he come. He's here already.

Slowly death turns up the lights from underneath, from the ground.
    The heath shines, a stronger and stronger purple –
no, a colour no one has seen . . . until the morning's pale light whines
    in through the eyelids

and I waken to that unshakeable PERHAPS that carries me through
    the wavering world.
And each abstract picture of the world is as impossible as the
    blue-print of a storm.

At home stood the all-knowing Encyclopedia, a yard of bookshelf, in
    it I learnt to read.
But each one of us has his own encyclopedia written, it grows out of
    each soul,

it's written from birth onwards, the hundreds of thousands of pages
    stand pressed against each other
and yet with air between them! Like the quivering leaves in a forest.
    The book of contradictions.

What's there changes by the hour, the pictures retouch themselves,
    the words flicker.
A wake washes through the whole text, it's followed by the next wave,
    and then the next . . .

From March 1979

Weary of all who come with words, words but no language
I make my way to the snow-covered island.
The untamed has no words.
The unwritten pages spread out on every side!
I come upon the tracks of deer's hooves in the snow.
Language but no words.

Memories Look at Me

A June morning, too soon to wake,
too late to fall asleep again.

I must go out – the greenery is dense
with memories, they follow me with their gaze.

They can't be seen, they merge completely with
the background, true chameleons.

They are so close that I can hear them breathe
although the birdsong here is deafening.

Winter's Gaze

I lean like a ladder and with my face
reach in to the second floor of the cherry tree.
I'm inside the bell of colours, it chimes with sunlight.
I polish off the swarthy red berries faster than four magpies.

A sudden chill, from a great distance, meets me.
The moment blackens
and remains like an axe-cut in a tree-trunk.

From now on it's late. We make off half-running
out of sight, down, down in the ancient sewage system.
The tunnels. We walk about there for months
half in service and half in flight.

Brief devotions when some hatchway opens above us
and a weak light falls.
We look up: the starry sky through the grating.

The Station

A train has just rolled in. Coach after coach stand here,
but no doors open, no one gets off or on.
Are there no doors at all? Inside, a crowd
of shut-in figures stirring to and fro.
Gazing out through immovable window-panes.
Outside, a man who walks along the coaches with a hammer.
He strikes the wheels, a feeble clang. Except for here!
Here the chime swells unbelievably: a lightning stroke,
peal of cathedral bells, a sailing-round-the-world peal
that lifts the whole train and the landscape's wet stones.
Everything is singing. This you will remember. Travel on!

Answers to Letters

In the bottom drawer of my desk I come across a letter that first arrived
twenty-six years ago. A letter in panic, and it's still breathing when it
arrives the second time.

A house has five windows: through four of them the day shines clear
and still. The fifth faces a black sky, thunder and storm. I stand at the
fifth window. The letter.

Sometimes an abyss opens between Tuesday and Wednesday but
twenty-six years may be passed in a moment. Time is not a straight
line, it's more of a labyrinth, and if you press close to the wall at the
right place you can hear the hurrying steps and the voices, you can hear
yourself walking past there on the other side.

Was the letter ever answered? I don't remember, it *was* long ago.
The countless thresholds of the sea went on migrating. The heart went
on leaping from second to second like the toad in the wet grass of an
August night.

The unanswered letters pile up, like cirro-stratus clouds promising bad weather. They make the sunbeams lustreless. One day I will answer. One day when I am dead and can at last concentrate. Or at least so far away from here that I can find myself again. When I'm walking, newly arrived, in the big city, on 125th Street, in the wind on the street of dancing garbage. I who love to stray off and vanish in the crowd, a capital T in the endless mass of the text.

Icelandic Hurricane

Not earth-tremor but sky-quake. Turner could have painted it, lashed tight. A solitary mitt has just whirled by, several miles from its hand. I am going to make my way against the wind to that house on the other side of the field. I flutter in the hurricane. I am X-rayed, the skeleton hands in its resignation. Panic grows as I beat upwind, I founder, I founder and drown on dry land! How heavy, everything I suddenly have to drag along, how heavy for the butterfly to tow a barge! There at last. A final wrestle with the door. And now inside. And now inside. Behind the big glass pane. What a strange and wonderful invention glass is – to be close yet untouched…Outside, a horde of transparent sprinters in giant format charges across the lava plain. But I'm no longer fluttering. I'm sitting behind the glass, at rest, my own portrait.

The Blue Wind-Flowers

To be spell-bound – nothing's easier. It's one of the oldest tricks of the soil and springtime: the blue wind-flowers. They are in a way unexpected. They shoot up out of the brown rustle of last year in overlooked places where one's gaze never pauses. They glimmer and float, yes, float, and that comes from their colour. That sharp violet-blue now weighs nothing. Here is ecstasy, but low-voiced. "Career" – irrelevant! "Power" and "publicity" – ridiculous! They must have laid on a great reception up in Nineveh, with pompe and "Trompe up!". Raising the rafters. And above all those brows the crowning crystal chandeliers hung like glass vultures. Instead of such an over-decorated and strident cul-de-sac, the wind-flowers open a secret passage to the real celebration, which is quiet as death.

The Blue House

It is a night of radiant sun. I stand in the dense forest and look away towards my house with its haze-blue walls. As if I had just died and was seeing the house from a new angle.

It has stood for more than eighty summers. Its wood is impregnated with four times joy and three times sorrow. When someone who lived in the house dies, it is repainted. The dead person himself is painting, without a brush, from inside.

Beyond the house, open ground. Once a garden, now grown over. Stationary breakers of weed, pagodas of weed, welling text, upanishads of weed, a viking fleet of weed, dragon-heads, lances, a weed-empire!

Across the overgrown garden there flutters the shadow of a boomerang that is thrown again and again. It has something to do with a person who lived in the house long before my time. Almost a child. An impulse comes from him, a thought, a thought like an act of will: 'make...draw...' To escape out of his fate.

The house is like a child's drawing. A deputising childishness that grew because someone – much too soon – gave up his mission to be a child. Open the door, step in! In here there's unrest in the ceiling and peace in the walls. Above the bed hangs a painting of a ship with seventeen sails, hissing wave-crests and a wind that the gilt frame can't contain.

It's always so early in here, before the crossroads, before the irrevocable choices. Thank you for this life! Still I miss the alternatives. The sketches, all of them, want to become real.

A motor far away on the water expands the summer-night horizon. Both joy and sorrow swell in the dew's magnifying glass. Without really knowing, we divine; our life has a sister ship, following quite another route. While the sun blazes behind the islands.

Satellite Eyes

The ground is rough, no mirror.
Only the coarsest of spirits
can reflect themselves there: the Moon
and the Ice Age.

Come closer in the dragon-haze!
Heavy clouds, milling streets.
A rustling downpour of souls.
Barrack-squares.

Nineteen Hundred and Eighty

His glance flits in jerks across the newsprint.
Feelings come, so icy they're taken for thoughts.
Only in deep hypnosis could he be his other I,
his hidden sister, the woman who joins the hundreds of thousands
screaming 'Death to the Shah!' – although he is already dead –
a marching black tent, pious and full of hate.
Jihad! Two who shall never meet take the world in hand.

Black Picture-Postcards

I

The diary written full, future unknown.
The cable hums the folk-song with no home.
Snow-fall on the lead-still sea. Shadows
                    wrestle on the pier.

II

In the middle of life it happens that death comes
and takes man's measurements. The visit
is forgotten and life goes on. But the suit
                        is sewn on the quiet.

Fire-Jottings

Throughout the dismal months my life sparkled alive only when I made
        love with you.
As the firefly ignites and fades out, ignites and fades out, – in glimpses
        we can trace its flight
in the dark among the olive trees.

Throughout the dismal months the soul lay shrunken, lifeless,
but the body went straight to you.
The night sky bellowed.
Stealthily we milked the cosmos and survived.

Many Steps

The icons are laid in the earth face up
and the earth trod down again
by wheels and shoes, by thousands of steps,
by the heavy steps of ten thousand doubters.

In my dream I stepped down into a luminous underground pool,
a surging litany.
What sharp longing! What idiotic hope!
And over me the tread of millions of doubters.

Postludium

I drag like a grapnel over the world's floor –
everything catches that I don't need.
Tired indignation. Glowing resignation.
The executioners fetch stone. God writes in the sand.

Silent rooms.
The furniture stands in the moonlight, ready to fly.
I walk slowly into myself
through a forest of empty suits of armour.

Dream Seminar

Four thousand million on earth.
They all sleep, they all dream.
Faces throng, and bodies, in each dream –
the dreamt-of people are more numerous
than us. But take no space . . .
You doze off at the theatre perhaps,
in mid-play your eyelids sink.
A fleeting double-exposure: the stage
before you out-manoeuvred by a dream.
Then no more stage, it's you.
The theatre in the honest depths!
The mystery of the overworked director!
Perpetual memorising of new plays . . .
A bedroom. Night.
The darkened sky is flowing through the room.
The book that someone fell asleep from lies
still open
sprawling wounded at the edge of the bed.
The sleeper's eyes are moving,
they're following the text without letters
in another book –
illuminated, old-fashioned, swift.
A dizzying commedia inscribed
within the eyelids' monastery walls.

A unique copy. Here, this very moment.
In the morning, wiped out.
The mystery of the great waste!
Annihilation. As when suspicious men
in uniforms stop the tourist –
open his camera, unwind the film
and let the daylight kill the pictures:
thus dreams are blackened by the light of day.
Annihilated or just invisible?
There is a kind of out-of-sight dreaming
that never stops. Light for other eyes.
A zone where creeping thoughts learn to walk.
Faces and forms regrouped.
We're moving on a street, among people
in blazing sun.
But just as many – maybe more –
we don't see
are also there in dark buildings
high on both sides.
Sometimes one of them comes to the window
and glances down on us.

Codex

Men of footnotes, not headlines. I find myself in the deep corridor
that would have been dark
if my right hand wasn't shining like a torch.
The light falls on something written on the wall
and I see it
as the diver sees the name on the sunken hull flimmering towards him
        in the flowing depths:
ADAM ILEBORGH 1448. Who?
It was he who made the organ spread its clumpy wings and rise –
and it held itself airborne nearly a minute.
An experiment blessed with success!
Written on the wall: MAYONE, DAUTHENDEY, KAMINSKY . . . The light
        touches name upon name.
The walls are quite scrawled over.

They're the names of the all-but extinct artists
the men of footnotes, the unplayed, the half-forgotten, the immortal
        unknown.
For a moment it feels as if they're all whispering their names at once –
whispering added to whispering till a tumbling breaker cascades along
        the corridor
without throwing anyone down.
Though the corridor is no longer a corridor.
Neither a graveyard nor a market-place but something of both.
A kind of green-house too.
Plenty of oxygen here.
Dead men of the footnotes can breathe deeply, they remain in the
        ecological system.
But there is much they are spared.
They are spared swallowing the morality of power,
they are spared the black-and-white chequered game where the smell
        of corpses is the only thing that never dies.
They are rehabilitated.
And those who can no longer receive
have not stopped giving.
They rolled out a little of the radiant and melancholy tapestry
and let go again.
Some are anonymous, they are my friends
without my knowing them, they are like those stone-people
carved on grave-slabs in old churches.
Soft or harsh reliefs in walls we brush against, figures and names
sunk in the stone floors, on the way to extinction.
But those who really want to be struck from the list . . .
They don't stop in the region of footnotes,
they step into the downward career that ends in oblivion and peace.
Total oblivion. It's a kind of exam
taken in silence: to step over the border without anyone noticing . . .

Carillon

Madame despises her guests because they want to stay at her shabby
    hotel.
I have the corner-room, one floor up: a wretched bed, a lightbulb in
    the ceiling.
Heavy drapes where a quarter of a million mites are on the march.

Outside, a pedestrian street
with slow tourists, hurrying school-children, men in working-clothes
    who wheel their rattling bikes.
Those who think they make the earth go round and those who think
    they go round helplessly in earth's grip.
A street we all walk, where does it emerge?

The room's only window faces something else: The Wild Market
    Square,
ground that seethes, a wide trembling surface, at times crowded and
    at times deserted.

What I carry within me is materialised there, all terrors, all expectations.
All the inconceivable that will nevertheless happen.

I have low beaches, if death rises six inches I shall be flooded.
I am Maximilian. It's 1488. I'm held prisoner here in Bruges
because my enemies are irresolute –
they are wicked idealists and what they did in horror's back-yard I can't
    describe, I can't turn blood into ink.

I am also the man in overalls wheeling his rattling bike down on the
    street.

I am also the person seen, that tourist, the one loitering and pausing,
    loitering and pausing
and letting his gaze wander over the pale moon-tanned faces and surging
    draperies of the old paintings.

No one decides where I go, least of all myself, though each step is where
    it must be.
Walking round in the fossil-wars where all are invulnerable because
    all are dead!

The dusty foliage, the walls with their loop-holes, the garden paths
 where petrified tears crunch under the heels . . .

Unexpectedly, as if I'd stepped on a trip-wire, the bell-ringing starts
 in the anonymous tower.
Carillon! The sack splits along its seams and the chimes roll out across
 Flanders.
Carillon! The cooing iron of the bells, hymn and hit-song in one, and
 tremblingly written in the air.
The shaky-handed doctor wrote out a prescription that no one can
 decipher but his writing will be recognised . . .

Over meadow and house-top, harvest and mart,
over quick and dead the carillon rings.
Christ and Antichrist, hard to tell apart!
The bells bear us home at last on their wings.

They have stopped.

I am back in the hotel room: the bed, the light, the drapes. There are
 strange noises, the cellar is dragging itself up the stairs.

I lie on the bed with my arms outstretched.
I am an anchor that has dug itself down and holds steady
the huge shadow floating up there,
the great unknown which I am a part of and which is certainly more
 important than me.

Outside, the walkway, the street where my steps die away and also what
 is written, my preface to silence and my inside-out psalm.

Molokai

We stand at the edge and deep down under us glisten the roofs of the
 leper colony.
The climb down we could manage but we'd never make it back up the
 slopes before nightfall.
So we turn back through the forest, walk among trees with long blue
 needles.

It's silent here, like the silence when the hawk is coming.
These are woods that forgive everything but forget nothing.
Damien, for love, chose life and obscurity. He received death and
    fame.
But we see these events from the wrong side: a heap of stones instead
    of the sphinx's face.

FOR LIVING AND DEAD

FÖR LEVANDE OCH DÖDA

(1989)

The Forgotten Captain

We have many shadows. I was walking home
in the September night when Y
climbed out of his grave after forty years
and kept me company.

At first he was quite empty, only a name
but his thoughts swam
faster than time ran
and caught up with us.

I put his eyes to my eyes
and saw war's ocean.
The last boat he captained
took shape beneath us.

Ahead and astern the Atlantic convoy crept,
the ships that would survive
and the ships that bore the Mark
(invisible to all)

while sleepless days and nights relieved each other
but never him.
Under his oilskin, his lifejacket.
He never came home.

It was an internal weeping that bled him to death
in a Cardiff hospital.
He could at last lie down
and turn into a horizon.

Goodbye, eleven-knot convoys! Goodbye, 1940!
Here ends world history.
The bombers were left hanging.
The heathery moors blossomed.

A photo from early this century shows a beach.
Six Sunday-best boys.
Sailing-boats in their arms.
What solemn airs!

The boats that became life and death for some of them.
And writing about the dead –
that too is a game, made heavy
with what is to come.

Six Winters

1

In the black hotel a child is asleep.
And outside: the winter night
where the wide-eyed dice roll.

2

An élite of the dead became stone
in Katarina Churchyard
where the wind shakes in its armour from Svalbard.

3

One wartime winter when I lay sick
a huge icicle grew outside the window.
Neighbour and harpoon, unexplained memory.

4

Ice hangs down from the roof-edge.
Icicles: the upside-down Gothic.
Abstract cattle, udders of glass.

5

On a side-track an empty railway carriage.
Still. Heraldic.
With the journeys in its claws.

6

Tonight snow-haze, moonlight. The moonlight jellyfish itself
is floating before us. Our smiles
on the way home. Bewitched avenue.

The Nightingale in Badelunda

In the green midnight at the nightingale's northern limit. Heavy
leaves hang in trance, the deaf cars race towards the neon-line.
The nightingale's voice rises without wavering to the side, it is as
penetrating as a cock-crow, but beautiful and free of vanity. I was
in prison and it visited me. I was sick and it visited me. I didn't
notice it then, but I do now. Time streams down from the sun and
the moon and into all the tick-tock-thankful clocks. But right here
there is no time. Only the nightingale's voice, the raw resonant
notes that whet the night sky's gleaming scythe.

Early May Stanzas

A May wood The invisible removal load,
   my whole life, like a haunting here. Birds in song.
      In the silent pools, midge-larvae –
         their dancing furious question-marks.

The same places I escape to, and the same words.
   Cool sea breeze. And the ice-dragon licks the back
      of my neck while sunlight blazes.
         The load is burning with chilly flames.

Berceuse

I am a mummy at rest in the blue coffin of the forests, in the
    perpetual roar of engines and rubber and asphalt.

What happened during the day sinks, the homework is heavier
    than life.

The wheelbarrow rolled forward on its single wheel and I myself
    travelled on my spinning psyche, but now my thoughts
    have stopped going round and the wheelbarrow has got
    wings.

At long last, when space is black, a plane will come. The passengers
    will see the cities beneath them glittering like the gold of
    the Goths.

Streets in Shanghai

1

The white butterfly in the park is read by many.
I love that cabbage-white as if it were a fluttering corner of truth
    itself!

At dawn the crowds get our silent planet going with their running.
The park fills with people. To each one there are eight faces
    polished like jade, for every situation, for the avoidance of
    mistakes.

To each one, also, the invisible face that mirrors 'something one
    doesn't talk about'.
Something that turns up in tired moments and is acrid like a
    mouthful of adder-brandy with its lingering scaly aftertaste.

The carp in the pond move perpetually, they swim while they
    sleep, they are models for the faithful: always in motion.

2

It's midday. The washing flutters in the grey sea-wind high above
        the cyclists
who come in dense shoals. Mind the labyrinths to left and right!

I'm surrounded by written signs I can't interpret, I'm totally
        illiterate.
But I've paid what I should and have receipts for everything.
I've accumulated about me so many illegible receipts.
I'm an old tree with withered leaves that hang on and can't fall to
        the earth.

And a puff of air from the sea makes all those receipts rustle.

3

At dawn the crowds get our silent planet going with their tramping.
We are all aboard the street. It is packed like the deck of a ferry.
Where are we going? Are there enough tea-cups? We can count
        ourselves lucky getting aboard this street!
It's a thousand years before the birth of claustrophobia.

Behind each one walking here there hovers a cross which wants to
        catch up on us, overtake us, unite with us.
Something which wants to creep up behind us and cover our eyes
        and whisper 'Guess who!'

We look almost happy out in the sun, while we are bleeding fatally
        from wounds we don't know about.

Deep in Europe

I a dark hull floating between two lock-gates
rest in the hotel bed while the city around me wakens.
The silent clamour and the grey light stream in
and raise me slowly to the next level: the morning.

Overheard horizon. They want to say something, the dead.
They smoke but don't eat, they don't breathe but still have their
        voices.
I'll be hurrying through the streets like one of them.
The blackened cathedral, heavy as a moon, causes ebb and flow.

Leaflet

The silent rage scribbles on the wall inwards.
Fruit trees in blossom, the cuckoo calls.
It's spring's narcosis. But the silent rage
paints its slogans backwards in the garages.

We see all and nothing, but straight as periscopes
wielded by the underground's shy crew.
It's the war of the minutes. The blazing sun
stands above the hospital, suffering's parking-place.

We living nails hammered down in society!
One day we shall loosen from everything.
We shall feel death's air under our wings
and become milder and wilder than here.

The Indoors is Endless

It's spring in 1827, Beethoven
hoists his death-mask and sails off.

The grindstones are turning in Europe's windmills.
The wild geese are flying northwards.

Here is the north, here is Stockholm
swimming palaces and hovels.

The logs in the royal fireplace
collapse from Attention to At Ease.

Peace prevails, vaccine and potatoes,
but the city wells breathe heavily.

Privy barrels in sedan chairs like paschas
are carried by night over the North Bridge.

The cobblestones make them stagger
mamselles loafers gentlemen.

Implacably still, the sign-board
with the smoking blackamoor.

So many islands, so much rowing
with invisible oars against the current!

The channels open up, April May
and sweet honey dribbling June.

The heat reaches islands far out.
The village doors are open, except one.

The snake-clock's pointer licks the silence.
The rock slopes glow with geology's patience.

It happened like this, or almost.
It is an obscure family tale

about Erik, done down by a curse
disabled by a bullet through the soul.

He went to town, met an enemy
and sailed home sick and grey.

Keeps to his bed all that summer.
The tools on the wall are in mourning.

He lies awake, hears the woolly flutter
of night moths, his moonlight comrades.

His strength ebbs out, he pushes in vain
against the iron-bound tomorrow.

And the God of the depths cries out of the depths
'Deliver me! Deliver yourself!'

All the surface action turns inwards.
He's taken apart, put together.

The wind rises and the wild rose bushes
catch on the fleeing light.

The future opens, he looks into
the self-rotating kaleidoscope

sees indistinct fluttering faces
family faces not yet born.

By mistake his gaze strikes me
as I walk around here in Washington

among grandiose houses where only
every second column bears weight.

White buildings in crematorium style
where the dream of the poor turns to ash.

The gentle downward slope gets steeper
and imperceptibly becomes an abyss.

Vermeer

No protected world...Just behind the wall the noise begins,
the inn is there
with laughter and bickering, rows of teeth, tears, the din of bells
and the insane brother-in-law, the death-bringer we all must
          tremble for.

The big explosion and the tramp of rescue arriving late
the boats preening themselves on the straits, the money creeping
          down in the wrong man's pocket
demands stacked on demands
gaping red flowerheads sweating premonitions of war.

In from there and right through the wall into the clear studio
into the second that's allowed to live for centuries.
Pictures that call themselves 'The Music Lesson'
or 'Woman in Blue Reading a Letter' –
she's in her eighth month, two hearts kicking inside her.
On the wall behind is a wrinkled map of Terra Incognita.

Breathe calmly...An unknown blue material is nailed to the chairs.
The gold studs flew in with incredible speed
and stopped abruptly
as if they had never been other than stillness.

Ears sing, from depth or height.
It's the pressure from the other side of the wall.
It makes each fact float
and steadies the brush.

It hurts to go through walls, it makes you ill
but is necessary
The world is one. But walls...
And the wall is part of yourself –
we know or we don't know but it's true for us all
except for small children. No walls for them.

The clear sky has leant against the wall.
It's like a prayer to the emptiness.
And the emptiness turns its face to us
and whispers
'I am not empty, I am open.'

Romanesque Arches

Inside the huge romanesque church the tourists jostled in the half
        darkness.
Vault gaped behind vault, no complete view.
A few candle-flames flickered.
An angel with no face embraced me
and whispered through my whole body:
'Don't be ashamed of being human, be proud!
Inside you vault opens behind vault endlessly.
You will never be complete, that's how it's meant to be.'
Blind with tears
I was pushed out on the sun-seething piazza
together with Mr and Mrs Jones, Mr Tanaka and Signora Sabatini
and inside them all vault opened behind vault endlessly.

Epigram

The buildings of capital, the hives of the killer bees, honey for the
        few.
He served there. But in a dark tunnel he unfolded his wings
and flew when no one was looking. He had to live his life again.

Female Portrait, 19th Century

Her voice is stifled in the clothing. Her eyes
follow the gladiator. Then she herself is
on the arena. Is she free? A gilt frame
                              strangles the picture.

Medieval Motif

Beneath our spell-binding play of faces there waits
inevitably the skull, the poker-face. While
the sun's unhurriedly rolling past in the sky.
                              And the chess continues.

A barber-scissor-like clipping sound from the copse.
The sun's unhurriedly rolling past in the sky.
The game of chess comes to a standstill, in a draw.
                              In the rainbow's silence.

Air Mail

On the hunt for a letter-box
I took the letter through the city.
In the big forest of stone and concrete
the straying butterfly flickered.

The flying-carpet of the stamp
the staggering lines of the address
plus my own sealed truth
soaring now over the ocean.

The Atlantic's creeping silver.
The cloud-banks. The fishing-boat
like a spat-out olive-stone.
And the pale scars of the wakes.

Down here work goes slowly.
I ogle the clock often.
The tree-shadows are black ciphers
in the greedy silence.

The truth's there, on the ground
but no one dares to take it.
The truth's there, on the street.
No one makes it his own.

Madrigal

I inherited a dark wood where I seldom go. But a day will come
when the dead and the living change places. The wood will be set
in motion. We are not without hope. The most serious crimes will
remain unsolved in spite of the efforts of many policemen. In the
same way there is somewhere in our lives a great unsolved love. I
inherited a dark wood, but today I'm walking in the other wood, the
light one. All the living creatures that sing, wriggle, wag and crawl!
It's spring and the air is very strong. I have graduated from the
university of oblivion and am as empty-handed as the shirt on the
washing-line.

Golden Wasp

The blindworm that legless lizard flows along the porch step
calm and majestic as an anaconda, only the size is different.
The sky is covered with clouds but the sun pushes through. Such
      is the day.

This morning the woman I love drove away the evil spirits.
As when you open the door of a dark shed somewhere in the south
and the light pours in
and the cockroaches dart off into the corners and up the walls
and are gone – you saw them and you didn't see them –
so her nakedness made the demons run.

As if they never existed.
But they'll come back.
With a thousand hands crossing the lines in the old-fashioned
      telephone exchange of the nerves.

It's the fifth of July. The lupins are stretching up as if they wanted
      to catch sight of the sea.
We're in the church of keeping-silence, of piety according to no
      letter.
As if they didn't exist, the implacable faces of the patriarchs
and the misspelling of God's name in stone.

I saw a true-to-the-letter TV preacher who'd piled in the money.
But he was weak now and needed the support of a bodyguard,
who was a well-tailored young man with a smile tight as a muzzle.
A smile stifling a scream.
The scream of a child left alone in a hospital bed when the parents
      leave.

The divine brushes against a human being and lights a flame
but then draws back.
Why?
The flame attracts the shadows, they fly rustling in and join the flame,
which rises and blackens. And the smoke spreads out black and
      strangling.
At last only the black smoke, at last only the pious executioner.

The pious executioner leans forward
over the market-place and the crowd that make a grainy mirror
where he can see himself.

The greatest fanatic is the greatest doubter. Without knowing it.
He is a pact between two
where the one is a hundred per cent visible and the other invisible.
How I hate that expression 'a hundred per cent'.

Those who can never exist anywhere except on their facades
those who are never absent-minded
those who never open the wrong door and catch a glimpse of the
          Unidentified One.
Walk past them!

It's the fifth of July. The sky is covered with clouds but the sun
          pushes through.
The blindworm flows along the porch step, calm and majestic as
          an anaconda.
The blindworm as if there were no bureaucracy.
The golden wasp as if there were no idolatry.
The lupins as if there were no 'hundred per cent'.

I know the depth where one is both prisoner and ruler, like
          Persephone.
I often lay in the stiff grass down there
and saw the earth arch over me.
The vault of the earth.
Often – that was half of my life.

But today my gaze has left me.
My blindness has gone away.
The dark bat has left my face and is scissoring around in summer's
          bright space.

THE SAD GONDOLA

SORGEGONDOLEN

(1996)

Note: From 19 November 1882 until 13 January 1883 Liszt stayed with his daughter Cosima and her husband Richard Wagner at the Palazzo Vendramin, on the Grand Canal in Venice. Inspired by the sight of funeral gondolas, and also 'under a premonition', Liszt wrote the two piano pieces *La lugubre gondola* I and II. Wagner died on 13 February.

April and Silence

Spring lies desolate.
The velvet-dark ditch
crawls by my side
without reflections.

The only thing that shines
is yellow flowers.

I am carried in my shadow
like a violin
in its black box.

The only thing I want to say
glitters out of reach
like the silver
in a pawnbroker's.

National Insecurity

The Under Secretary leans forward and draws an X
and her ear-drops dangle like swords of Damocles.

As a mottled butterfly is invisible against the ground
so the demon merges with the opened newspaper.

A helmet worn by no one has taken power.
The mother-turtle flees flying under the water.

A Page of the Night-Book

I stepped ashore one May night
in the cool moonshine
where grass and flowers were grey
but the scent green.

I glided up the slope
in the colour-blind night
while white stones
signalled to the moon.

A period of time
a few minutes long
fifty-eight years wide.

And behind me
beyond the lead-shimmering waters
was the other shore
and those who ruled.

People with a future
instead of a face.

The Sad Gondola

I

Two old men, father-in-law and son-in-law, Liszt and Wagner,
        are staying by the Grand Canal
together with the restless woman who married King Midas
the man who transforms everything he touches into Wagner.
The green chill of the sea forces its way up through the palace
        floors.
Wagner is marked, the well-known Mr Punch profile is wearier
        than before
the face a white flag.
The gondola is heavily laden with their lives, two returns and one
        single.

II

One of the palace windows flies open and the people inside
        grimace in the sudden draught.
Outside on the water the garbage gondola appears, paddled by
        two one-oared bandits.
Liszt has written down some chords that are so heavy they ought
        to be sent
to the mineralogical institute in Padua for analysis.
Meteorites!
too heavy to rest, they can only sink and sink through the
        future right down
to the years of the brownshirts.
The gondola is heavily laden with the crouching stones of the
        future.

III

Peep-holes, opening on 1990.

March 25. Anxiety over Lithuania.
Dreamt that I visited a large hospital.
No staff. Everyone a patient.

In the same dream a new-born girl
who spoke in complete sentences.

IV

Beside his son-in-law, who is a man of the age, Liszt is a moth-
        eaten Grand Seigneur.
It's a disguise.
The deep that tries on and rejects different masks has picked out
        this one for him.
The deep that wants to step in, to visit the humans, without
        showing its face.

V

Abbé Liszt is accustomed to carrying his own suitcase through
        slush and sunshine
and when the time comes to die no one will meet him at the
        station.
A warm breeze of highly-gifted brandy carries him off in the
        middle of some task.
He is never free of tasks.
Two thousand letters per year!
The schoolboy writing out the wrongly-spelt word a hundred
        times before he can go home.
The gondola is heavily laden with life, it is simple and black.

VI

1990 again.

Dreamt that I drove 200 kilometres for nothing.
Then everything grew large. Sparrows
big as hens sang deafeningly.

Dreamt that I drew piano keys
on the kitchen table. I played on them, silently.
The neighbours came in to listen.

VII

The keyboard which has kept silent through the whole of *Parsifal*
          (but it has listened) is at last allowed to say something.
Sighs...sospiri...
When Liszt plays this evening he holds down the sea-pedal
so that the green power of the sea rises through the floor and
          merges with the stonework of the building.
Good evening, beautiful deep!
The gondola is heavily laden with life, it is simple and black.

VIII

Dreamt that I was to start school but came late.
Everyone in the room was wearing a white mask.
Impossible to tell who the teacher was.

Landscape with Suns

The sun emerges round the house
stands in the middle of the road
and breathes on us
with its red blast.
Innsbrück I must leave you.
But tomorrow
there will be a glowing sun
in the half-dead grey forest
where we have to work and live.

November in the Former DDR

The almighty cyclop's-eye clouded over
and the grass shook itself in the coal dust.

Beaten black and blue by the night's dreams
we board the train
that stops at every station
and lays eggs.

Almost silent.
The clang of the church bells' buckets
fetching water.
And someone's inexorable cough
scolding everything and everyone.

A stone idol moves its lips:
it's the city.
Ruled by iron-hard misunderstandings
among kiosk attendants butchers
metal-workers naval officers
iron-hard misunderstandings, academics!

How sore my eyes are!
They've been reading by the faint glimmer of the glow-worm
        lamps.

November offers caramels of granite.
Unpredictable!
Like world history
laughing at the wrong place.

But we hear the clang
of the church bells' buckets fetching water
every Wednesday
– is it Wednesday? –
so much for our Sundays!

From July 1990

It was a funeral
and I felt that the dead man
was reading my thoughts
better than I could.

The organ was silent, the birds sang.
The grave out in the sunshine.
My friend's voice belonged
on the far side of the minutes.

I drove home seen-through
by the glitter of the summer day
by rain and quietness
seen-through by the moon.

The Cuckoo

A cuckoo sat hoo-hooing in the birch just north of the house. It
was so loud that at first I thought it was an opera-singer doing a
cuckoo-imitation. I looked at the bird in surprise. Its tail feathers
moved up and down to each note like a pump-handle. The bird
was bouncing on both feet, turning round and screaming towards
every point of the compass. Then it took off, muttering, and flew
over the house off to the west... Summer is growing old and every-
thing is flowing into a single melancholy murmur. *Cuculus canorus*
will return to the tropics. Its time in Sweden is over. Its time here
was not long! In fact the cuckoo is a citizen of Zaire... I am no
longer so fond of making journeys. But the journey visits me. Now
when I am more and more pushed into a corner, when the annual
growth-rings multiply, when I need reading-glasses. Always there
is much more happening than we can bear. There is nothing to be
surprised at. These thoughts bear me as faithfully as Susi and
Chuma bore Livingstone's embalmed body right through Africa.

Three Stanzas

I

The knight and his lady
turned to stone but happy
on a flying coffin-lid
outside time.

II

Jesus held up a coin
with Tiberius in profile
a profile without love
power in circulation.

III

A dripping sword
wipes out the memories.
On the ground trumpets
and sword-belts rust.

Like Being a Child

Like being a child and a sudden insult
is jerked over your head like a sack
through its mesh you catch a glimpse of the sun
and hear the cherry trees humming.

No help in that – the great insult
covers your head your torso your knees
you can move sporadically
but can't look forward to spring.

Glimmering woolly hat, pull it down over your face
stare through the stitches.
On the straits the water-rings are crowding soundlessly.
Green leaves are darkening the earth.

Two Cities

Each on its side of a strait, two cities
the one blacked out, occupied by the enemy.
In the other the lamps are burning.
The bright shore hypnotises the dark one.

I swim out in a trance
on the glittering dark waters.
A dull tuba-blast penetrates.
It's a friend's voice, take up your grave and walk.

The Light Streams In

Outside the window, the long beast of spring
the transparent dragon of sunlight
rushes past like an endless
suburban train – we never got a glimpse of its head.

The shoreline villas shuffle sideways
they are proud as crabs.
The sun makes the statues blink.

The raging sea of fire out in space
is transformed to a caress.
The countdown has begun.

Night Journey

Thronging under us. The trains.
Hotel Astoria trembles.
A glass of water at the bedside
shines in the tunnels.

He dreamt he was a prisoner on Svalbard.
The planet turned rumbling.
Glittering eyes walked over the ice-fields.
The beauty of miracles existed.

Haiku

The power lines stretched
across the kingdom of frost
north of all music.

                *

The white sun's a long-
distance runner against
the blue mountains of death.

                *

We have to live with
the small-print grasses and
laughter from the cellar.

                *

The sun is low now.
Our shadows are giants.
Soon all will be shadow.

                *

The purple orchids.
Oil-tankers are gliding past.
The moon's at the full.

                *

Medieval keep.
Alien city, cold sphinx,
empty arenas.

                *

The leaves whispering:
a wild boar's at the organ.
And the bells pealed out.

                *

The night flows westwards
horizon to horizon
all at the moon's speed.

                *

The presence of God.
In the tunnel of birdsong
a locked seal opens.

                *

Oak-trees and the moon.
Light. Silent constellations.
And the cold ocean.

From the Island, 1860

I

One day as she rinsed clothes from the jetty
the chill of the strait rose through her arms
into her life.

Her tears froze into a pair of glasses.
The island raised itself in the grass
and the banner of Baltic herring swayed in the depths.

II

And the swarm of smallpox caught up with him
clustered onto his face.
He lies and stares at the ceiling.

What plying of oars up the silence.
The moment's eternally running stain
the moment's eternally bleeding point.

Silence

Walk past, they are buried...
A cloud glides across the sun's disk.

Starvation is a tall building
that moves by night

in the bedroom a lift-shaft opens
it's a dark rod pointing to the inner domains.

Flowers in the ditch. Fanfare and silence.
Walk past, they are buried...

The table-silver survives in big shoals
deep down where the Atlantic is black.

Midwinter

A blue sheen
radiates from my clothes.
Midwinter.
Jangling tambourines of ice.
I close my eyes.
There is a soundless world
there is a crack
where dead people
are smuggled across the border.

A Sketch from 1844

William Turner's face is weather-brown
he has set up his easel far out among the breakers.
We follow the silver-green cable down in the depths.

He wades out in the shelving kingdom of death.
A train rolls in. Come closer.
Rain, rain travels over us.

MEMORIES LOOK AT ME
AUTOBIOGRAPHICAL CHAPTERS

Memories

'My life.' Thinking these words, I see before me a streak of light. On closer inspection it has the form of a comet, with head and tail. The brightest end, the head, is childhood and growing up. The nucleus, the densest part, is infancy, that first period, in which the most important features of our life are determined. I try to remember, I try to penetrate there. But it is difficult to move in these concentrated regions, it is dangerous, it feels as if I am coming close to death itself. Further back, the comet thins out – that's the longer part, the tail. It becomes more and more sparse, but also broader. I am now far out in the comet's tail, I am sixty as I write this.

Our earliest experiences are for the most part inaccessible. Retellings, memories of memories, reconstructions based on moods that suddenly flare into life.

My earliest datable memory is a feeling. A feeling of pride. I have just turned three and it has been declared that this is very significant, that I am now big. I'm in bed in a bright room, then clamber down to the floor stunningly aware of the fact that I am becoming a grown-up. I have a doll to whom I gave the most beautiful name I could think of: Karin Spinna. I don't treat her in a motherly fashion. She is more like a comrade or someone I am in love with.

We live in Stockholm, in the Söder area, at Swedenborgsgatan 33 (now called Grindsgatan). Father is still part of the family but is soon to leave. Our ways are quite "modern" – right from the start I use the familiar *du* form to my parents. My mother's parents are close by, just round the corner, in Blekingegatan.

My maternal grandfather, Carl Helmer Westerberg, was born in 1860. He was a ship's pilot and a very good friend of mine, seventy-one years older than myself. Oddly enough, there was the same difference in age between him and his own maternal grandfather, who was born in 1789: the storming of the Bastille, the Anjala mutiny, Mozart writing his clarinet quintet. Two equal steps back in time, two long steps, yet not really so very long. We can touch history.

Grandfather's way of speech belonged to the nineteenth century. Many of his expressions would today seem surprisingly old-fashioned. But in his mouth, and to my ear, they felt altogether natural. He was a fairly short man, with a white moustache and a prominent and rather crooked nose – 'like a Turk's,' as he said. His tempera

ment was lively and he could flare up. His occasional outbursts
were never taken too seriously and they were over as soon as they
had begun. He was quite without aggression of the insistent kind.
Indeed he was so conciliatory that he risked being labelled as soft.
He wanted to keep on the best side even of people who might be
criticised – in their absence – in the course of ordinary conversa-
tion. 'But surely you must agree that X is a crook!' 'Well, well –
that's something I don't really know about...'

After the divorce, mother and I moved to Folkungagatan 57, a
lower-middle-class tenement. A motley crowd lived there in close
proximity to each other. My memories of life there arrange them-
selves like scenes from a film of the thirties or the forties, with the
appropriate list of characters. The lovable concierge, her strong
laconic husband whom I admired because, among other things, he
had been poisoned by gas and that suggested a heroic closeness to
dangerous machines.

There was a trickle of comers and goers who didn't belong there.
The occasional drunk would slowly return to his wits on the stair-
way. Several times a week beggars would ring. They would stand
there in the porch mumbling. Mother made sandwiches for them
– she gave them slices of bread rather than money.

We lived on the fifth floor. At the top, that is. There were four
doors, plus the entry to the attic. On one of them was the name
Orke, press photographer. In a way it seemed grand to live beside
a press photographer.

Our immediate neighbour, the one we heard through the wall,
was a bachelor, well into middle age, yellowish complexion. He
worked at home, running some sort of broker's business by phone.
In the course of his calls he often gave vent to hilarious guffaws
that burst through the walls into our flat. Another recurring sound
was the pop of corks. Beer bottles did not have metal caps then.
Those Dionysiac sounds, the guffaws of laughter and the popping
of corks, seemed hardly to belong to the spectrally pale old fellow
sometimes met in the lift. As the years passed he became suspicious
and the bouts of laughter diminished in frequency.

Once there was an outbreak of violence. I was quite small. A
ghbour had been shut out by his wife; he was drunk and furious
he had barricaded herself in. He tried to break down the door
vled out various threats. What I remember is that he screamed
iar sentence: 'I don't give a damn if I go to Kungsholmen!'
ther what he meant, about Kungsholmen. She explained
ce headquarters was there. And that part of town then

acquired a sense of something fearful. (That was a feeling inten-sified when I visited St Erik's Hospital and saw the war-wounded from Finland who were cared for there in the winter of 1939-40.)

Mother left for work early in the morning. She didn't take a tram or bus – throughout her entire adult life she walked to and fro between Söder and Östermalm – she worked in the Hedvig Leonora School and was in charge of the third and fourth classes year after year. She was a devoted teacher and greatly involved with the children. One might imagine it would be hard for her to accept retirement. But it wasn't – she felt greatly relieved.

Since mother worked we had a home-help, a 'maid' as she was called, though 'child-minder' would have been nearer the truth. She slept in a minimal room which was really part of the kitchen and which was not included in the official flat-with-two-rooms-and-kitchen designation of our home.

When I was five or six, our maid was called Anna-Lisa and she came from Eslöv, in Skåne in the south of Sweden. I thought she was very attractive: blond frizzy hair, a turned-up nose, a mild Skåne accent. She was a lovely person and I still feel something special when I pass Eslöv station. But I have never actually stepped off the train at that magic place.

She was particularly talented at drawing. Disney figures were her specialty. I myself drew almost uninterruptedly throughout those years, in the late 1930s. Grandfather brought home rolls of brown paper of the sort then used in all the grocery shops, and I filled the sheets with illustrated stories. I had, to be sure, taught myself to write at the age of five. But it was too slow a process. My imagination needed some speedier means of expression. I didn't even have enough patience to draw properly. I developed a kind of shorthand sketching method with figures in violent move-ment, breakneck drama yet no details. Cartoon strips consumed only by myself.

One day in the mid-1930s I disappeared in the middle of Stock-holm. Mother and I had been to a school concert. In the crush by the exit I lost my grasp of her hand. I was carried helplessly away by the human current and since I was so small I could not be dis-covered. Darkness was falling over Hötorget. I stood there, robbed of all sense of security. There were people around me but they were intent on their own business. There was nothing to hold on to. It was my first experience of death.

After an initial period of panic I began to think. It should be possible to walk home. It was absolutely possible. We had come by

bus. I had knelt on the seat as I usually did and looked out of the
bus window. Drottninggatan had flowed past. What I had to do now,
simply, was to walk back the same way, bus stop by bus stop.

I went in the right direction. Of that long walk I have a clear
memory of only one part – of reaching Norrbro and seeing the
water under the bridge. The traffic here was heavy and I didn't
dare set off across the street. I turned to a man who was standing
beside me and said: 'There's a lot of traffic here.' He took me by
the hand and led me across.

But then he let go of me. I don't know why this man and all
the other unknown adults thought it was quite in order for a little
boy to wander by himself through Stockholm on a dark evening.
But that's how it was. The remainder of the journey – through
Gamla Stan, the old town, over Slussen and into Söder – must
have been complicated. Perhaps I homed in on my destination with
the help of the same mysterious compass that dogs and carrier
pigeons have in them – no matter where they are released they
always find the way home. I remember nothing of that part. Well,
yes, I do – I remember how my self-confidence grew and grew so
that when I did at last arrive home I was quite euphoric. Grand-
father met me. My devastated mother was sitting in the police
station following the progress of the search for me. Grandfather's
firm nerves didn't fail him; he received me quite naturally. He
was glad of course, but didn't make a fuss. It all felt secure and
natural.

Museums

As a child I was attracted to museums. First, the Natural History Museum. What a building! Gigantic, Babylonian, inexhaustible! On the ground floor, hall after hall where stuffed mammals and birds thronged in the dust. And the arches, smelling of bones, where the whales hung from the roof. Then one floor up: the fossils, the invertebrates...

I was taken to the Natural History Museum when I was only about five years old. At the entrance, two elephant skeletons met the visitor. They were the two guardians at the gateway to the miraculous. They made an overwhelming impression on me and I drew them in a big sketchbook.

After a time those visits to the Natural History Museum stopped. I was going through a phase when I was quite terrified of skeletons. The worst was the bony figure depicted at the end of the article on 'Man' in the Nordic Family Lexicon. But my fear was aroused by skeletons in general, including the elephant skeletons at the entrance to the museum. I became frightened even of my own drawing of them and couldn't bring myself to open the sketchbook.

My interest now turned to the Railway Museum. Nowadays it occupies spacious premises just outside the town of Gävle but then the entire museum was squeezed into a part of the district of Klara right in the centre of Stockholm. Twice a week grandfather and I made our way down from Söder and visited the museum. Grandfather must himself have been enthralled by the model trains, otherwise he would hardly have endured so many visits. When we decided to make a day of it we would finish up in Stockholm Central Station, which was nearby, and watch the trains come steaming in, full-sized.

The museum staff noticed the zeal of the young boy and on one occasion I was taken into the museum office and allowed to write my name (with a back-to-front S) in a visitors' book. I wanted to be a railway engineer. I was, however, more interested in steam engines than in electric ones. In other words, I was more romantic than technical.

Some time later, as a schoolboy, I returned to the Natural History Museum. I was now an amateur zoologist, solemn, like a little professor. I sat bent over the books about insects and fish.

I had started my own collections. They were kept at home in a cupboard. But inside my skull there grew up an immense museum and a kind of interplay developed between this imaginary one and the very real one which I visited.

I went out to the Natural History Museum more or less every second Sunday. I took the tram to Roslagstull and walked the rest. The road was always a little longer than I had imagined. I remember those foot marches very clearly: it was always windy, my nose ran, my eyes filled with tears. I don't remember the journeys in the opposite direction. It's as if I never went home, only out to the museum, a sniffling, tearful, hopeful expedition towards a giant Babylonian building.

Finally arriving, I would be greeted by the elephant skeletons. I often went directly to the "old" part, with animals which had been stuffed away back in the eighteenth century, some of them rather clumsily prepared, with swollen heads. Yet there was a special magic there. Big artificial landscapes with elegantly designed and positioned animal models failed to catch my interest – they were make-believe, something for children. No, it had to be quite clear that this was not a matter of living animals. They were stuffed, they stood there in the service of science. The scientific method I was closest to was the Linnean: discover, collect, examine.

I would work through the museum. Long pauses among the whales and in the palaeontology rooms. And then the part which detained me most of all: the invertebrates.

I never had any contact with other visitors. In fact, I don't remember there being other visitors at all. Other museums which I occasionally visited – the National Maritime Museum, the National Museum of Ethnography, the Museum of Technology – were always crowded. But the Natural History Museum seemed to stay open only for me.

One day I did encounter someone – no, not a visitor, he was a professor or something like that – working in the museum. We met among the invertebrates – he suddenly materialised between the showcases, and was almost as small in stature as I was. He spoke half to himself. At once we were involved in a discussion of molluscs. He was so absent-minded or so unprejudiced that he treated me like an adult. One of those guardian angels who appeared now and then in my childhood and touched me with its wings.

Our conversation resulted in my being allowed into a section of the museum that was not open to the public. I was given much good advice on the preparation of small animals, and was equipped with little glass tubes which seemed to me truly professional.

I collected insects, above all beetles, from the age of eleven until I had turned fifteen. Then other, competing, interests, mostly artistic, forced their attentions on me. How melancholy it felt, that entomology must give way! I convinced myself that this was only a temporary adjustment. In fifty years or so I would resume my collecting.

The activity began in the spring and then flourished of course in the summer, out on the island of Runmarö. In the summerhouse, where we had little enough space to move around in, there stood jam jars with dead insects and a display board for butterflies. And lingering everywhere: the smell of ethyl acetate, a smell I carried with me since I always had a tin of the insect killer in my pocket.

It would no doubt have been more daring to use potassium cyanide as the handbook recommended. Fortunately that substance was not within my reach and so I never had to test my courage by choosing whether or not to use it.

Many were involved in the insect hunt. The neighbourhood children learnt to sound the alarm when they saw some insect that could be of interest. 'Here's one!!' echoed among the houses, and I would come rushing along with the butterfly net.

I was out on endless expeditions. A life in the open air without the slightest thought of thereby improving my health. I had no aesthetic opinions on my booty, of course – this was, after all, Science – but I absorbed unawares many experiences of natural beauty. I moved in the great mystery. I learnt that the ground was alive, that there was an infinite world of creeping and flying things living their own rich life without paying the least regard to us.

I caught a fraction of a fraction of that world and pinned it down in my boxes, which I still have. A hidden mini-museum of which I am seldom conscious. But they're sitting there, those insects. As if they were biding their time.

Primary School

I began in Katarina Norra Primary School and my teacher was Miss R, a tidy spinster who changed her clothes every day. As school ended each Saturday, each child was given a caramel, but otherwise she was often strict. She was generous when it came to pulling hair and delivering blows, although she never hit me. I was the son of a teacher.

My chief task that first term was to sit still at my desk. I could already write and count. I was allowed to sit and cut out shapes in coloured paper, but what the shapes were I can't remember.

I have a feeling that the atmosphere was fairly good throughout my first year there but that it chilled somewhat as time passed. Any disturbance to good order, any hitches or snags, made Miss R lose her temper. We were not allowed to be restless or loud-voiced. We were not to whine. We were not to experience unexpected difficulties in learning something. Above all, we were not to do anything unexpected. Any little child who wet himself or herself in shame and fear could hope for no mercy.

As I said, being the son of a teacher saved me from blows. But I could feel the oppressive atmosphere generated by all those threats and reproaches. In the background there was always the head teacher, a hawk-nosed dangerous character. The very worst prospect was to be sent to a reform school, something which would be mentioned on special occasions. I never felt this as a threat to me personally but the very idea gave a disagreeable sensation.

I could well imagine what a reformatory was like, the more so since I'd heard the name of one – 'Skrubba' ('Scrub'), a name suggesting rasps and planes. I took it as self-evident that the inmates were subjected to daily torture. The world view which I had acquired allowed for the existence of special institutions where adults tortured children – perhaps to death – for having been noisy. That was dreadful. but so must it be. If we were noisy, then…

When a boy from our school was taken to a reformatory and then returned after a year there, I regarded him as someone who had risen from the dead.

A more realistic threat was evacuation. During the first years of the war, plans were made for the evacuation of all schoolchildren from the bigger cities. Mother wrote the name TRANSTRÖMER with marking ink on our sheets and so on. The question was whether I would be evacuated with mother and her school class or with my own class from Katarina Norra, i.e., deported with Miss R. I suspected the latter.

I escaped evacuation. Life at school went on. I spent all my time in school longing for the day to come to an end so that I could throw myself into what really interested me: Africa, the underwater world, the Middle Ages, etc. The only thing which really caught my attention in school was the wall charts. I was a devotee of wall charts. My greatest happiness was to accompany teacher to the storeroom to fetch some worn cardboard chart. While doing so I could peep at the other ones hanging there. I tried to make some at home, as best I could.

One important difference between my life and that of my class-mates was that I could not produce any father. The majority of my class came from working–class families where divorce was clearly something very rare. I would never admit that there was anything peculiar about my domestic situation. Not even to myself. No, of course I had a father, even if I met him only once a year (usually on Christmas Eve), and I kept track of him – at one point during the war he was, for example, on a torpedo boat and he sent me an amusing letter. I would have liked to have shown this letter in class but the right chance never came.

I remember a moment of panic. I had been absent for a couple of days and when I came back a classmate told me that the teacher – not Miss R but a substitute – had said to the class that they must not tease me on account of the fact that I had no father. In other words, they were sorry for me. I panicked, hearing that. I was obviously abnormal. I tried to talk it all away, my face bright red.

I was acutely aware of the danger of being regarded as an out-sider because at heart I suspected I was one. I was absorbed in interests which no normal boy would have. I joined a drawing class, voluntarily, and sketched underwater scenes: fish, sea urchins, crabs, shells. Teacher remarked out loud that my drawings were very 'special' and my panic returned. There was a kind of insensi-tive adult who always wanted to point me out as somehow odd. My classmates were really more tolerant. I was neither popular nor bullied.

Hasse, a big darkish boy who was five times stronger than I was, had a habit of wrestling with me every break during our first year at school. At first I resisted violently but that got me nowhere for he just put me to the ground anyway and triumphed over me. At last I thought up a way of disappointing him: total relaxation. When he approached me I pretended that my Real Self had flown away leaving only a corpse behind, a lifeless rag which he could press to the ground as he wished. He soon grew tired of that.

I wonder what this method of turning myself into a lifeless rag can have meant for me further on in life. The art of being ridden roughshod over while yet maintaining one's self-respect. Have I resorted to the trick too often? Sometimes it works, sometimes not.

The War

It was the spring of 1940. I was a skinny nine-year-old stooped over the newspaper, intent on the war map where black arrows indicated the advance of the German tank divisions. Those arrows penetrated France and for us, Hitler's enemies, they lived as parasites in our bodies. I really counted myself as one of Hitler's enemies. My political engagement has never been so wholehearted!

To write of the political engagement of a nine-year-old no doubt invites derision, but this was hardly a question of politics in the proper sense of the word. It meant simply that I took part in the war. I hadn't the slightest conception of matters such as social problems, classes, trade unions, the economy, the distribution of resources, the rival claims of socialism and capitalism. A 'Communist' was someone who supported Russia. 'Right-wing' was a shady term because some of those at that end of the political spectrum had German leanings. My further understanding of 'Right-wing' was that one voted in that direction if one were rich. Yet what did it really mean to be rich ? On a few occasions we were invited for a meal with a family who were described as rich. They lived in Äppelviken and the master of the house was a wholesale dealer. A large villa, servants in black and white. I noticed that the boy in the family – he was my age – had an incredibly big toy car, a fire engine, highly desirable. How did one get hold of such a thing? I had a momentary glimpse of the idea that the family belonged to a different social class, one in which people could afford unusually large toy cars. That is still an isolated and not very important memory.

Another memory: during a visit home with a classmate it surprised me that there was no WC, only a dry closet out in the backyard, like the kind we had in the country. We would pee into a discarded saucepan which my friend's mother would swill down the kitchen sink. It was picturesque detail. On the whole it didn't occur to me that the family lacked this or that. And the villa in Äppelvik did not strike me as remarkable. I was far short of the capacity which many seem to have acquired even in their early years of grasping the class status and economic level of a given environment merely at a glance. Many children seemed able to do so, not I.

My 'political' instincts were directed entirely at the war and Nazism. I believed one was either a Nazi or an anti-Nazi. I had no understanding of that lukewarm attitude, that opportunistic wait-and-see stance which was widespread in Sweden. I interpreted that

either as support for the Allies or as covert Nazism. When I realised
that some person I liked was really 'pro-German', I immediately
felt a terrible tightening over my breast. Everything was ruined.
There could never be any kind of fellow feeling between us.

From those close to me I expected unequivocal support. One
evening when we were on a visit to Uncle Elof and Aunt Agda,
the news inspired my generally taciturn uncle to comment that
'the English are successfully retreating...' He said this almost with
regret yet it struck me there was an ironic undertone (on the whole
irony was foreign to him) and I suddenly felt that tightening. The
Allied version of history was never questioned. I stared grimly up
at the roof light. There was consolation to be found there. It had
the shape of a British steel helmet: like a soup plate.

On Sundays we often had dinner in Enskede with my other
uncle and aunt on Mother's side; they provided a sort of support
family for Mother after the divorce. It was part of the ritual there
to turn on the BBC's Swedish broadcast on the radio. I shall never
forget the programme's opening flourish: first the victory signal
and then the signature tune, which was alleged to be 'Purcell's
Trumpet Voluntary' but which in fact was a rather puffed-up
arrangement of a harpsichord piece by Jeremiah Clarke. The
announcer's calm voice, with a shade of accent, spoke directly to
me from a world of friendly heroes who saw to it that it was busi-
ness as usual even if bombs were raining down.

When we were on the suburban train on the way to Enskede I
always wanted Mother – who hated attracting attention – to unfold
the propaganda paper *News from Great Britain*, and thus silently make
public our stance. She did nearly everything for me, including that.

I seldom met Father during the war. But one day he popped
up and took me off to a party with his journalist friends. The
glasses were standing ready, there were voices and laughter and
the cigarette smoke was dense. I went round being introduced and
answering questions. There was a relaxed and tolerant atmosphere
and I could do what I wanted. I withdrew by myself and sidled
along the bookshelves of this strange house.

I came across a newly published book called *The Martyrdom of
Poland*. Documentary. I settled on the floor and read it just about
cover to cover while the voices filled the air. That terrible book –
which I have never seen again – contained what I feared, or per-
haps what I hoped for. The Nazis were as inhuman as I had
imagined, no, they were worse! I read fascinated and disturbed
and at the same time a feeling of triumph emerged: I'd been right!

It was all in the book, the proof was there. Just wait! One day this
will be revealed, one day all of you who have doubted will have
the truth thrown in your faces. Just wait! And that in the event is
what happened.

Libraries

'Medborgarhuset' (*lit.* 'The Citizens' House') was built around 1940. A big four-square block in the middle of Söder, but also a bright and promising edifice, modern, 'functional'. It was only five minutes from where we lived.

In it there were, among other things, a public swimming pool and a branch of the city library. The children's section was, by obvious natural necessity, my allotted sphere, and to begin with it did have books enough for my consumption. The most important was Brehm's *Lives of the Animals*.

I slipped into the library nearly every day. But this was not an entirely trouble-free process. It sometimes happened that I tried to borrow books which the library ladies did not consider suitable for my age. One was Knut Holmboe's violent documentary *The Desert Is Burning*.

'Who is to have this book?'

'I am...'

'Oh no...'

'I...'

'You can tell your dad he can come and borrow it himself.'

It was even worse when I tried to get into the adult section. I needed a book which was definitely not to be found in the children's section. I was stopped at the entrance.

'How old are you?'

'Eleven.'

'You can't borrow books here. You can come back in a few years.'

'Yes, but the book I want is only in here.'

'What book?'

'*The Animals of Scandinavia: A History of Their Migration*.' And I added 'by Ekman', in hollow tones, feeling the game was lost. It was. Out of the question. I blushed, I was furious. I would never forgive her!

In the meantime my uncle of few words – Uncle Elof – intervened. He gave me his card to the adult section and we maintained the fiction that I was collecting books for him. I could now get in where I wanted.

The adult section shared a wall with the pool. At the entry one felt the fumes from within, the chlorine smell came through the ventilation system and the echoing voices could be heard as from a distance. Swimming pools and suchlike always have strange

acoustics. The temple of health and the temple of books were neigh-
bours, a good idea. I was a faithful visitor to the Medborgarhus
branch of the city library for many years. I regarded it as clearly
superior to the central library up on Sveavägen – where the atmo-
sphere was heavier and the air was still, no fumes of chlorine, no
echoing voices. The books themselves had a different smell there;
it gave me headaches.

Once given a free run of the library I devoted my attention mostly
to non-fiction. I left literature to its fate. Likewise the shelves
marked Economics and Social Problems. History, though, was
interesting. Medicine scared me.

But it was Geography that was my favourite corner. I was a
special devotee of the Africa shelf, which was extensive. I can
recall titles like *Mount Elgon, A Market-Boy in Africa, Desert
Sketches...* I wonder if any of the books which then filled the shelf
are still there.

Someone called Albert Schweitzer had written a book enticingly
called *Between Water and Primeval Forest*. It consisted mostly of
speculations about life. But Schweitzer himself stayed put in his
mission and didn't move, he wasn't a proper explorer. Not like,
for instance, Gösta Moberg, who covered endless miles (why?) in
alluring, unknown regions, such as Niger or Chad, lands about which
there was scant information in the library. Kenya and 'Tanganyika'
however were favoured on account of their Swedish settlements.
Tourists who sailed up the Nile to the Sudd area and then turned
north again – they wrote books. But none of those who ventured
into the arid zones of the Sudan, none of those who made their
way into Kordofan or Dar Fur. The Portuguese colonies of Angola
and Mozambique, that looked so big on the map, were also unknown
and neglected areas on the Africa shelf – and that made them even
more attractive.

I read a lot of books standing there in the library – I didn't want
to take home too many books of the same kind, or the same book
several times in succession. I felt I would be criticised by one or
other of the library staff and that was something to be avoided at
all costs.

One summer – I don't remember which one – I lived through
an elaborate and persistent daydream about Africa. That was out
on the island of Runmarö, a long way from the library. I withdrew
into a fantasy – I was leading an expedition right through central
Africa. I trudged on through the woods of Runmarö and kept
track of roughly how far I'd gone with a dotted line on a big map

of Africa, a map of the whole of Africa which I had drawn. If I worked out, for instance, that in the course of a week I had walked 120 kilometres on Runmarö, I marked in 120 kilometres on the map. It wasn't much.

At first I'd thought of starting the expedition on the east coast, more or less where Stanley had begun. But that would have left much too great a distance to traverse before I could reach the most interesting parts. I changed my mind and imagined that I travelled as far as Albert Nyansa by car. And that was where the expedition proper started, on foot. I would then have at least a reasonable chance of putting most of the Ituri Forest behind me before summer ended.

It was a nineteenth-century expedition, with bearers, etc. I was half aware, though, that this was now an obsolete way of travelling. Africa had changed. There was war in British Somaliland; it was in the news. Tanks were in action. It was indeed the first area where the Allies could claim an advance – I took due note of that, of course – and Abyssinia was the first country to be liberated from the Axis powers.

When my Africa dream returned several years later, it had been modernised and was now almost realistic. I was thinking of becoming an entomologist and collecting insects in Africa, discovering new species instead of new deserts.

Grammar School

Only a couple of my classmates from primary school progressed to secondary school ('realskola'). And no one apart from myself applied to Södra Latin Grammar School.

There was an entrance exam I had to sit. My sole memory of that is that I spelled the word 'särskilt' ('especially') wrongly, I gave it two *l*s. From then on the word had a disturbing effect on me which persisted far into the 1960s.

I have a distinct memory of my first day at Södra Latin in the autumn of 1942. It is as follows. I find myself surrounded by a number of unknown eleven-year-old boys. I have butterflies in my stomach, I'm uncertain and alone. But some of the others seem to know each other well – those are the pupils from Maria Preparatory. I look and look for a face from Katarina Norra. My mood consists of about equal parts of gloomy unease and hopeful expectation.

Our names are called out and we are divided into three classes. I am assigned to Class 15B and told to follow Dr Mohlin, who is to be our class teacher. One of the oldest teachers. His subject is German. He is small, with a sort of cat-like authority. He moves swiftly and quietly, he has bristly, reluctantly greying hair, and a bald wedge above each temple. From someone nearby who seems to know him, I catch an assessment of him: Målle – as he is called – is 'strict but fair'. Ominous.

From the first moment it was clear that grammar school was something quite different from primary school. Södra Latin was throughout masculine, the school was as single-sexed as a monastery or barracks. It was not until several years later that a couple of women were smuggled into the staff.

Each morning we all assembled in the school hall, sang hymns, and listened to a sermon delivered by one of the religious studies teachers. Then we marched off to our respective classrooms. The collective atmosphere of Södra Latin was immortalised by Ingmar Bergman in his film *Hets*.[1] (It was shot in the school and those of us who were pupils then appear as extras in several parts of the film.)

We were all supplied with a school manual which included, among other items, 'Directives as to order and discipline, in accordance with the school's statutes':

The pupils shall attend instruction at the determined times, neatly and decently attired and in possession of the necessary textbooks. They shall observe good order and proper conduct and shall follow the instruction with due attention. The pupils shall likewise attend morning devotions and there deport themselves quietly and attentively...

Pupils shall give due respect and obedience to the staff of the institution and shall accept with compliance their commands, corrections, and chastisements...

Södra Latin occupied the highest site on Söder, and its playground formed a plateau above most of the district's rooftops. The bricks of the school building could be seen from far away. The route to this castle of sighs was one I generally completed at a half-run. I hurried along by the long piles of wood – a sign of the crisis years – in front of 'Björns Trädgård', made my way up Götgatan – past Hansson and Bruce's bookshop – swung to the left into Höbergsgatan and there, every winter morning, stood a horse chewing straw in a nosebag. It was a brewery horse, a big steaming Ardenne. For a moment I found myself in its reeking shadow and the memory of that patient beast and of its smell in the cold and damp is still vivid. A smell that was at once suffocating and comforting.

I would rush into the playground just as the bells began to summon us to morning service. I was hardly ever late, for everything between the hours of eight and nine in the morning was well-timed. The spring was firm and tense as the school day began.

The end of the day at school was of course more relaxed, less regulated. Sometimes I went home with Palle. He was my closest friend in my first year at Södra Latin. We had quite a lot in common: his father, a sailor, was absent for long periods, and he was the only child of a good-natured mother who seemed pleased to see me. Palle had developed many of the characteristics of a single child, as I had, and he lived for his interests. He was above all a collector. Of what? Anything. Beer labels, matchboxes, swords, flint axes, stamps, postcards, shells, ethnographic oddments, and bones.

In his home, which was crammed full of his booty, we would duel with the swords. Together we carried out excavations at a secret spot on Riddarholmen and managed to retrieve bits of skeleton which my dentist identified as 'parts of a human being'.

Having Palle as a friend was an enriching experience but gradually we drifted apart. Further on in school Palle came to be absent for long periods because of illness. When he was transferred to another class we lost touch. My old friend was very far away. In fact he was marked by death. He appeared at school now only occasionally, pale and serious, with one leg amputated. When he died I found it impossible to accept. I developed a bad conscience but refused to recognise it. It felt as if I ought to suppress the memory of all the fun we'd had.

I feel I'm the same age as Palle, who died forty-five years ago without having grown up. But my old teachers, the 'oldies' as they were collectively termed, remain old in my memory in spite of the fact that the older among them were about the same age as I am now as I write this. We always feel younger than we are. I carry inside myself my earlier faces, as a tree contains its rings. The sum of them is 'me'. The mirror sees only my latest face, while I know all my previous ones.

The teachers who stand out in my memory are of course those who generated tension or excitement, those who were vivid, colourful, original. They were not in the majority but there was a fair number of them. There was something tragic about some of them, which we were able to sense. A critical situation which could be described thus: 'I know I can't be loved by those enviable turnip-heads in front of me. I know I can't be loved but at least I can make sure I won't be forgotten!'

The classroom was a theatre. The leading player, the teacher, performed on the stage, subjected to merciless scrutiny. The pupils were the audience and sometimes – one at a time – they would act a part as well.

We had to be on our guard, unfailingly. I had to get used to the recurring outbursts of aggression. Miss R had laid a good foundation – she had been strict and heavy-handed. Yet not really theatrical. At home there was nothing for me to learn in that direction. There were virtually no scenes at home, no rows, no bellowing father figure. Mother was spontaneous but undramatic. Giving vent to anger was childish. I had often been furious as a child but now I was a reasonably balanced youngster. My ideals were English – a stiff upper lip and so on. Outbursts of rage belonged to the Axis Powers.

At school there were choleric prima donnas who could devote most of a lesson to building up a tower of hysterical indignation, with the sole purpose of then emptying their vessels of wrath.

My class teacher Målle was hardly a prima donna. But he was the victim of a periodical and irresistible fury. Målle was really a charming person and a good teacher in his more harmonious periods. But, unhappily, what I remember best is that fury. Possibly the more violent outbursts did not come more often than three or four times a month. But it was upon those occasions that his great authority undoubtedly rested.

In the course of such lessons the thunder rolled to and fro across the landscape. That lightning would strike was clear to everyone, but no one could predict where. Målle did not victimise certain pupils. He was 'strict but fair'. Anyone might be struck by the lightning.

One day the lightning struck me. We were told to open our German grammars. I couldn't find mine. Was it in my schoolbag? Forgotten at home? I was lost. I couldn't find it.

'Stand up!'

I saw Målle dancing down from his desk and closing in on me. It was like being out in a field watching a bull approach.

The cuffs rained on me. I staggered this way and that. The next moment Målle was back sitting at his desk, frothing with rage, writing out a note for home. It was worded rather vaguely, accusing me of having been 'careless during a lesson' or something like that.

Many of the teachers hoped that those written notes home would lead to interrogations and the infliction of further punishments at the hands of parents.

Not so with us. Mother listened to my story, took the note and signed it. She noticed then that I had blue marks on my face, caused by the ringed hand of the pedagogue. Her reaction was unexpectedly strong. She said she would contact the school, per-haps ring the headmaster.

To which I protested. She couldn't do that! Everything had turned out OK. But now 'scandal' threatened. I would be called a mummy's boy and then persecuted forever, not just by Målle but by the entire staff.

She dropped the idea of course. And throughout my school days I made a point of keeping the two worlds – of school and of home – apart. If the two worlds were to seep into each other, then home would feel polluted. I would no longer have any proper refuge. Even today I find something disagreeable in the phrase 'co-operation between home and school'. I can see also that this holding apart of the separate worlds which I practised gave rise in due course to a more deliberately maintained distinction between private life and society. (This has nothing to do with political inclinations, whether to the left or to the right.) What we live through in school is projected as an image of society. My total experience of school was mixed, with more darkness than light. Just as my image of society has become. (Although we could well ask what we mean by 'society'.)

Contact between teacher and pupil was intensely personal and important personal characteristics were magnified in the classroom atmosphere as the result of the many tense situations. Personal, yes, but not in the slightest private. We knew virtually nothing about the private lives of our teachers although most of them lived in the streets around the school. There were, naturally, rumours – e.g., that Målle had been a featherweight boxer in his youth – but they were feebly supported by proper evidence and we scarcely gave them credit. We had trustworthy information about two of the most discreet younger teachers, men who never inspired any drama. One of them, allegedly, was poor and eked out his salary by playing the piano in a restaurant in the evenings. He had been seen. The other, allegedly, was a chess champion. That had been in the newspaper.

One day in the autumn Målle came into a lesson with a *Russula aerugina* in his hand. He set the mushroom on his desk. It was both liberating and shocking to have caught a glimpse of his private life! We knew now that Målle gathered mushrooms.

None of the teachers expressed political opinions. But at that time there were of course unprecedented tensions in the staff room. The Second World War was being fought out there too. Many of the teachers were convinced Nazis. As late as 1944 one of them, it was said, exclaimed in the staff room, 'If Hitler falls then *I* shall fall!' He didn't fall, however. I had him in German later. He recovered so well that he was able to welcome Hesse's Nobel Prize in 1946 with triumphant bellowing.

I was a worthy pupil but not one of the best. Biology ought to have been my favourite subject, but for most of my secondary schooling I had a biology teacher who really was too odd. At some point in the past he had blotted his copybook hopelessly, he had been warned and was now like a quenched volcano. My best subjects were geography and history. There I had an assistant teacher called Brännman, ruddy, energetic, a youngish man whose straight blond hair had a tendency to stand on end when he got angry, which happened quite often. He had plenty of goodwill and I liked him. The essays I wrote were always on geographical or historical subjects. They were long. On that point I heard a story much later from another Södra Latin pupil, Bo Grandien.[2] Bo became a close friend of mine in the later years of school but what he told me related to an earlier year when we didn't know each other.

He said that the first time he heard me mentioned was as he passed some of my classmates in one of the breaks. They had just been given back their essays and were dissatisfied with their grades. Bo heard the indignant remark: 'We can't *all* write *as fast* as Tranan, can we?' [3]

Bo decided that 'Tranan' was a detestable character who ought to be avoided. To me, this story is in a way comforting. Nowadays well-known for deficient productivity, I was then clearly noted as a prolific scribbler, someone who sinned through excessive productivity, a literal Stakhanov.

1. *Hets* – in Britain the film was called *Frenzy,* and in the USA, *Torment.*
2. Poet and journalist (*b.* 1932).
3. 'Tranan': the crane (the bird).

Exorcism

During the winter when I was fifteen I was afflicted by a severe form of anxiety. I was trapped by a searchlight which radiated not light but darkness. I was caught each afternoon as twilight fell and not released from that terrible grip until next day dawned. I slept very little, I sat up in bed, usually with a thick book before me. I read several thick books in that period but I can't say I really read them for they left no trace in my memory. The books were a pretext for leaving the light on.

It began in late autumn. One evening I'd gone to the cinema and seen *Squandered Days*, a film about an alcoholic. He finishes in a state of delirium – a harrowing sequence which today I would perhaps find rather childish. But not then.

As I lay down to sleep I reran the film in my mind's eye, as one does after being at the cinema.

Suddenly the atmosphere in the room was tense with dread. Something took total possession of me. Suddenly my body started shaking, especially my legs. I was a clockwork toy which had been wound up and now rattled and jumped helplessly. The cramps were quite beyond the control of my will, I had never experienced anything like this. I screamed for help and Mother came through. Gradually the cramps ebbed out. And did not return. But my dread intensified and from dusk to dawn would not leave me alone. The feeling that dominated my nights was the terror which Fritz Lang came near to catching in certain scenes of *Dr Mabuse's Testament*, especially the opening scene – a print works where someone hides while the machines and everything else vibrate. I recognised myself in this immediately, although my nights were quieter.

The most important element in my existence was *Illness*. The world was a vast hospital. I saw before me human beings deformed in body and in soul. The light burned and tried to hold off the terrible faces but sometimes I would doze off, my eyelids would close, and the terrible faces would suddenly be closing in on me.

It all happened in silence, yet within the silence voices were endlessly busy. The wallpaper pattern made faces. Now and then the silence would be broken by a ticking in the walls. Produced by what? By whom? By me? The walls crackled because my sick thoughts wanted them to. So much the worse... Was I insane? Almost.

I was afraid of drifting into madness but in general I did not feel threatened by any kind of illness – it was scarcely a case of hypochondria – but it was rather the total power of illness that aroused terror. As in a film where an innocuous apartment interior changes its character entirely when ominous music is heard, I now experienced the outer world quite differently because it included my awareness of that domination wielded by sickness. A few years previously I had wanted to be an explorer. Now I had pushed my way into an unknown country where I had never wanted to be. I had discovered an evil power. Or rather, the evil power had discovered me.

I read recently about some teenagers who lost all their joy in living because they became obsessed with the idea that AIDS had taken over the world. They would have understood me.

Mother had witnessed the cramps I suffered that evening in late autumn as my crisis began. But after that she had to be held outside it all. Everyone had to be excluded, what was going on was just too terrible to be talked about. I was surrounded by ghosts. I myself was a ghost. A ghost that walked to school every morning and sat through the lessons without revealing its secret. School had become a breathing space, my dread wasn't the same there. It was my private life that was haunted. Everything was upside down.

At that time I was sceptical towards all forms of religion and I certainly said no prayers. If the crisis had arisen a few years later I would have been able to experience it as a revelation, something that would rouse me, like Siddhartha's four encounters (with an old person, with a sick person, with a corpse, and with a begging monk). I would have managed to feel a little more sympathy for and a little less dread of the deformed and the sick who invaded my nocturnal consciousness. But then, caught in my dread, religiously coloured explanations were not available to me. No prayers, but attempts at exorcism by way of music. It was during that period I began to hammer at the piano in earnest.

And all the time I was growing. At the beginning of that autumn term I was one of the smallest in the class, but by its end I was one of the tallest. As if the dread I lived in were a kind of fertiliser helping the plant to shoot up.

Winter moved towards its end and the days lengthened. Now, miraculously, the darkness in my own life withdrew. It happened gradually and I was slow in realising fully what was happening. One spring evening I discovered that all my terrors were now marginal. I sat with some friends philosophising and smoking cigars. It was time to walk home through the pale spring night and I had no feeling at all of terrors waiting for me at home.

Still, it is something I have taken part in. Possibly my most important experience. But it came to an end. I thought it was Inferno but it was Purgatory.

Latin

In the autumn of 1946 I entered the Latin division of senior secondary school (upper high school). This meant new teachers: instead of Målle, Satan, Slöman (*slö* = dull) and Company came characters like Fjalar, Fido, Lillan ('the littl'un'), Moster ('Auntie') and Bocken ('The Buck'). The last of these was the most important because he was my class teacher and came to influence me more than I would have been willing to admit then as our personalities clashed.

A few years previously we had had a moment or two of dramatic contact, before he became my teacher, that is. I was late one day and came running along one of the school corridors. Another boy came hurtling in the opposite direction towards me. This was G., who belonged to a parallel class and was well known as a bully. We screeched to a halt, face to face, without managing quite to avoid a collision. This sudden braking generated a lot of aggression and we were alone in the corridor. G. took the chance offered – his right fist slammed into my midriff. My sight blackened and I fell to the floor, moaning like a ma'm'selle in a nineteenth-century novel. G. vanished.

As the darkness cleared I found myself staring up at a figure stooping over me. A drawn out, whining, singing voice kept repeating as if in despair, 'What's the matter? What's the matter?' I saw a pink face and very neatly trimmed chalkwhite beard. The expression on the face was worried.

That voice, that face, belonged to the Latin and Greek teacher Per Venström, alias Pelle Vänster (*vänster* = left), alias Bocken. Fortunately he refrained from any kind of interrogation as to why I was lying in a clutter on the floor, and he seemed satisfied when he saw I could walk away unaided. Since he showed himself to be worried and almost helpful, I formed the impression that Bocken was at heart a well-meaning person. Something of that impression persisted later as well, even when we had our conflicts.

Bocken's appearance was stylish, quite theatrical indeed. He usually accompanied his white beard with a dark wide-brimmed hat and a short cloak. A minimum of outdoor clothes in winter. An obvious touch of Dracula. At a distance he was superior and decorative, close up his face often had something helpless about it.

The half singing intonation which characterised him was a personal elaboration of the Gotland dialect.

Bocken suffered from a chronic arthritic condition and had an emphatic limp, yet he managed to move swiftly. He always made a dramatic entry into the classroom, throwing his briefcase onto his desk; then, after a few seconds, we knew without doubt whether his mood was favourable or stormy. The state of the weather evidently affected his mood. On cool days his lessons could be downright jovial. When an area of low pressure hovered over us and the skies were cloudy, his lessons crawled along in a dull and fretful atmosphere punctuated by those inescapable outbursts of rage.

He belonged to the category of human being which it was quite impossible to imagine in a role other than that of schoolteacher. It could be said indeed that it was hard to envisage him as anything other than a Latin teacher.

In the course of my penultimate year at school, my own brand of modernistic poetry was in production. At the same time I was drawn to older poetry, and when our Latin lessons moved forward from the historical texts on wars, senators, and consuls to verses by Catullus and Horace, I was carried quite willingly into the poetic world presided over by Bocken.

Plodding through verses was educative. It went like this. The pupils first had to read out a stanza, from Horace perhaps:

> Aequam memento rebus in arduis
> servare mentem, non secus in bonis
>   ab insolenti temperatam
>   laetitia, morituri Delli

Bocken would cry out: 'Translate!' And the pupil would oblige:

> With an even temper...aah...Remember that in an even temper... no... with equanimity...to maintain an even temper in difficult conditions, and not otherwise...aah...and like in fav-...favourable conditions...aah... abstain from excessive...aah...vivacious joy O mortal Dellius...

By now the luminous Roman text had really been brought down to earth. But in the next moment, in the next stanza, Horace came back in Latin with the miraculous precision of his verse. This alternation between the trivial and decrepit on the one hand and the buoyant and sublime on the other taught me a lot. It had to do with the conditions of poetry and of life. It was through form that something could be raised to another level. The caterpillar feet were gone, the wings unfolded. One should never lose hope!

Alas, Bocken never realised how captivated I was by those classical stanzas. To him I was a quietly provocative schoolboy whose incomprehensible nineteen-fortyish poems appeared in the school magazine – that was in the autumn of 1948. When he saw my efforts, with their consistent avoidance of capitals and punctuation marks, he reacted with indignation. I was to be identified as part of the advancing tide of barbarism. Such a person must be utterly immune to Horace.

His image of me was tarnished further after a lesson in which we were going through a medieval Latin text dealing with life in the thirteenth century. It was an overcast day; Bocken was in pain, and some kind of rage was just waiting to explode. Suddenly he tossed out the question— who was Erik the Lame Lisper? Erik had been referred to in our text. I replied that he was the founder of Grönköping.[1] This was a reflex action on my part coming from my wish to lighten the oppressive atmosphere. But Bocken was angry, not simply there and then but even at the end of term when I was given a 'warning'. This was a brief written message home to the effect that the pupil had been negligent in the subject, in this case Latin. Since my grades for written work were all high, this 'warning' presumably had to be seen with reference to life in general rather than to my performance in Latin.

In my last year at school our relationship was better. By the time I took my exams it was quite cordial.

Round about then two Horatian stanza forms, the sapphic and the alcaic, began to find their way into my own writing. In the summer after matriculation I wrote two poems in sapphic stanzas. The one was 'Ode to Thoreau', later pruned down to 'Five Stanzas to Thoreau', the more juvenile parts having been erased. The other was 'Storm', in the sequence 'Autumnal Archipelago'. But I don't know if Bocken ever acquainted himself with these. Classical metres – how did I come to use them? The idea simply turned up. For I regarded Horace as a contemporary. He was like René Char, Loerke, or Einar Malm. It was so naïve that it became sophisticated.

---

1. The archetypal smalltown. According to the satirical weekly *Grönköpings Veckoblad* the town was founded by King Erik Eriksson (1216-1250), known as Erik the Lame Lisper.

Index of titles and first lines